THE POETIC ART OF

W. H. AUDEN

THE POETIC ART OF
W. H. AUDEN

BY JOHN G. BLAIR

PRINCETON, NEW JERSEY

PRINCETON UNIVERSITY PRESS

1965

for $KARIN$ *and*
ANN

PREFACE

MANY people have contributed to the making of this book. I think with particular gratitude of Professor Leicester Bradner of Brown University and his former colleague, now President of Bucknell University, Charles H. Watts II, who together first opened my eyes to the life there is in literature. Professor Hyatt Waggoner of Brown, by his example, demonstrated the competence every serious piece of criticism must aim for. Professor Robert Creed of the same institution, acute teacher and critic, stimulated me to think and write better than I thought I could. Professor Edward Callan of Western Michigan University both in his writings and in his person revealed much to me about Auden's poetry and the profundity of his grasp of human nature.

Individuals associated with my own institution, Oakland University, have furthered my project in many ways. My senior colleague, Professor Robert Hoopes, Chairman of the Department of English, has played a crucial role in the preparation of this book. His comments have been both considerate and incisive. For having helped me learn things about Auden I might well have missed, I am grateful to the students in my seminar on Auden and those who made a success of the staged reading of *For the Time Being* held on the campus on March 22, 1964. Completion of the manuscript was supported by an Oakland Faculty Research Grant. Marian Wilson, editorial secretary, contributed immensely to this book by her continual acts of kindness and her competence.

I want to express my thanks also for the resources put at my disposal by a number of libraries: the Houghton Library at Harvard, the Lockwood Memorial Library at the University of Buffalo, the Newberry Library in Chicago, the Public Libraries of Boston, New York, and Detroit, the libraries of the University of Cincinnati, Wayne State University, Columbia University, Oakland University, and most especially the Brown University Library and its Harris Collection of American Poetry, Plays, and Music. Mr. Roger Stoddard, former classmate and Curator of the Collection, was particularly helpful.

Dr. John Drew O'Neill, now at the University of Michigan, created an exceptionally useful index.

My especial gratitude goes to Mr. Auden for his generosity with his time and his unfailing courtesy in answering questions during two interviews in March 1961, and January 1962.

I owe most of all to my wife, who, through the force of her ideas and the irreverence of her criticisms, measurably sharpened this book.

J.G.B.

Oakland University
Rochester, Michigan
August 1964

CONTENTS

THE POETIC ART OF
W. H. AUDEN

INTRODUCTION

THE major failing of Auden criticism to date results from a refusal to look at the art of his poetry as distinguished from the ideas it expresses or implies. Critics have created and maintained a poetically misleading division of Auden's work based on his move to America and his return to Christianity in the years 1939-1940. The majority of existing criticism divides itself with unfortunate neatness into three categories. First is commentary from a defensively "English" point of view; these critics, and especially reviewers, find that the quality of Auden's work has visibly declined since he emigrated from England. As of 1960, for example, Philip Larkin finds 1940 an unbridgeable gap in Auden's work. Before then he was a "tremendously exciting English social poet full of energetic unliterary knockabout and unique lucidity of phrase." Since 1940 his has been "an engaging, bookish, American talent, too verbose to be memorable and too intellectual to be moving."[1] Second, humanist critics conclude that Auden's poetry disintegrated once his religious position became orthodox. Joseph Warren Beach, for example, scorns Auden's reconversion in these terms: "Once again, as so often before, a hopeful generation realized that the millennium had failed to materialize. And once again, in discouragement, a generation abjured as unworkable the gospel of secular humanism. They decided that what they were taught in Sunday School must be right."[2] Third, applying an opposite but equally restrictive point of view are the self-consciously Christian commentators who wel-

[1] "What's Become of Wystan?" *Spectator*, ccv, No. 6890 (July 15, 1960), 104.
[2] "The Poems of Auden and the Prose Diathesis," *Virginia Quarterly Review*, xxv (Summer 1949), 370.

come Auden to the fold but ignore his earlier work. Even Nathan Scott, Jr., in a recent evaluation, considers Auden to have been a major poet only for the last twenty years— in other words since his reconversion to Christianity.[8]

Perhaps criticism based on polemic distinctions is inevitable during the early years of an author's acceptance as a major artist, but Auden, after all, has been publishing memorable poems for more than thirty-five years. Through these years the *poetic* phenomenon of W. H. Auden has rarely received primary attention. Fortunately, the elucidation of Auden's art has moved forward recently with the appearance of an important book by Monroe K. Spears, *The Poetry of W. H. Auden* (Oxford University Press, 1963). This careful and detailed rehearsal of Auden's unfolding career does group his work into segments but avoids the prejudicial insistence on "periods." In effect, Mr. Spears's sympathetic and lucid description of just what Auden has been doing in the world of poetry makes publicly available the raw material for a critical study like the present one. My interest is in building out of an informed familiarity with Auden's work a sense of the fundamental aesthetic attitudes and practices that have guided his poetry to date. To the grasping of characteristics common to a man's art throughout his career, "periods" are largely irrelevant. So are changes in political, philosophical, or religious profession. Consequently, this study makes reference to changes in Auden's intellectual stance only when these seem helpful in elucidating developments within his poetic practice.

When they have not dissected Auden's poetry by periods, critics before Mr. Spears have tended to evaluate

[8] "The Poetry of Auden," *The London Magazine*, VIII (January 1961), 44. Also in *Chicago Review*, XIII (Winter 1959), 53.

his work by standards that are misleading if not irrelevant. The commentary of Joseph Warren Beach has been prominent here. Auden's obvious versatility has led Mr. Beach to suggest that Auden's work is so various as to raise "a question of identity": "In a work of art, as in a man, we are best satisfied when we are confidently aware of a wholeness, or integrality, that underlies all the diverse and even conflicting elements. And we are most satisfied when there is a consistent thread running through the whole course of a man's life or the whole body of an artist's work."[4] The demand for wholeness or consistency is appropriate and reasonable, except when the critic insists that he will set the terms within which the poet must be consistent. That he should find Auden an unpredictable performer is implicit in Beach's neo-Romantic point of view as a critic. For example, he approves of poems like "Journey to Iceland" and "September 1, 1939" because "they are earnest, direct, and manly in their rendering of the poet's sentiments."[5] But the point of view which sees poetry as direct self-expression is bound to overlook something in the work of a poet who is as uncompromisingly indirect, theatrical, even "anti-Romantic" as Auden. This study tries to consider the poet's own intentions as part of its own critical point of view.

In fairness to Beach's observation, we can agree that Auden has made himself the master of many styles of poetry and that, on first glance, his work does seem bewilderingly diverse. Anyone who has attempted to parody the Auden "manner" has discovered the difficulty of pinning it down. William Empson's "Just a Smack at Au-

[4] *The Making of the Auden Canon* (Minneapolis, 1957), 253.
[5] *Ibid.*, 247.

den,"[6] written about 1937, is able to fix and parody only two prominent elements of Auden's practice to that time: rhetorically balanced balladeering and the prophecy of doom for contemporary English society. Even in the relatively small amount of verse Auden had published by 1937 there are numerous devices inviting parody: the suppression of articles and connectives, the reliance on half-rimes apparently inspired by Wilfred Owen, the use of a landscape of abandoned mines and traction engines. Since Empson's poem Auden has continued to try out new styles ranging from the prose of Henry James's late works to nursery rimes after Edward Lear. Between them there is enough to require a volume of parodies if we would hope to capture Auden's "manner."

Nonetheless, encouraged by Auden's own suggestion in 1962 that his "notions of what poetry should be are still, in all essentials, what they were"[7] in the late 1920's, I am convinced that there is a fundamental wholeness and consistency in his poetry—considered as poetry. Obviously, contradictions abound in the shifting themes and poetic styles that are so prominent at first glance. But in the poetic means he has brought to bear on basic artistic problems, Auden has been consistent enough to justify speaking of his characteristic "mode" of poetry, as opposed to his various "manners." In the body of Auden's work to date one can observe similarities of poetic attack and intent that are, in effect, predispositions of his imagination. There have been some relocations within Auden's mode, as we shall see, but these are fewer and less radical than appear at first. Auden is, from first

---

[6] *Collected Poems of William Empson* (New York, 1949), 64-65.
[7] *The Dyer's Hand* (New York, 1962), 278. Hereafter cited as DH.

to last, a moralist who wants his poems to arouse his audience into critical self-awareness and to incite them to reform. Yet he rejects all attempts, including some of his own early sermonizing, to tell the reader exactly what the moral truth is. He writes impersonal, often allegorical poems. They ask to be taken seriously not because they are the products of W. H. Auden but because they are just, incisive, and memorable mirrors for the reader's own condition as a human being. Auden tests his poems not for their openness of self-revelation but for their effect on his audience. A case in point is the alphabetical arrangement of short poems in the 1945 *Collected Poetry*. It is as though Auden was anticipating a desire in some of his readers to categorize his poems by periods while remaining unmoved by them. Analogous effects appear in the texture of his poems. Instead of connotative word-magic, he relies on "hard" diction. With the exception of some earlier works, his images do not seem to grow in any "organic" way, but to be constructed by a penetratingly intellectual imagination. Metaphors do not contain higher meanings within themselves as symbols; they demonstrate with striking particularity the renewed relevance of a general or abstract concept, which could be, and perhaps was, arrived at independently of the poem. If a single word can be made to categorize this mode, I think it should be "anti-Romantic." Characteristics such as these clearly do outline a path which is legitimate for a poetry, though not the kind of poetry many critics have asked it to be.

This analysis, then, seeks to isolate Auden's mode by exploring first the anti-Romantic impulses motivating his work, particularly as they appear in the restricted didacticism of his poetic theory. The study proceeds by distinguishing several ways his imagination habitually works to implement his didactic intentions: his use of allegory to bridge the fissure between public and private worlds, his reliance on dramatic or quasi-dramatic conventions to objectify and particularize his themes, and his choice of complex poetic forms and light verse techniques to cajole or trick the reader's consciousness—and perhaps Auden's—into a fresh encounter with himself. In Auden's contribution to the art of opera, I find a final epitomizing figure for his poetic mode.

In these pages appear many quotations from Auden's voluminous prose. Not only is Auden a reader of impressively catholic taste, but his fresh and responsive commentaries are delightful. He is a good critic, whose strong theoretical bent leads him toward generalizations about literature and writers more than toward specific poetic exegeses. Just because he is a good critic, because his criticism makes public what his unique and personal vision sees in the work at hand, his critical comments often reveal much about his own poems. To deny the relevance of his habits of mind as a critic would be to refuse important corroborating evidence for the way his imagination works.

In seeking to describe Auden's mode, this study follows a formula he developed in his own critical practice: "What kind of writing is this, as compared with other kinds? What are its special virtues and its special limitations? Judged by its own intentions, what makes one . . . better or worse than another?"[8] Clearly, the final judgment sought is a limited one: what can Auden's mode do especially well and what less than well? An attempt

[8] "The Wish Game," *New Yorker*, xxxiii (March 16, 1957), 139-140. *DH*, 211.

to evaluate the ultimate importance of Auden's poetry would be futile at this point. Now in his late fifties, the poet continues to grow in stature as an artist. Even now his substantial body of work reveals brilliant facility with words and profound insights into the nature of man.

This study indirectly demonstrates Auden's stature as a major poet, but, before entertaining its generalizations, the reader must be reminded of an essential qualification: there is always a danger that the critic may be trapped by his own very necessary ability to generalize. The reader must constantly return to the poetry itself for clarification and emendation. A responsive reading of Auden's work itself amply demonstrates his place in the tradition of great moral and philosophical poets in English. He has moral acuity worthy of a Langland, a Spenser, or a Milton, mated with the wit and facility of a Dryden, a Pope, or a Byron. Auden's ability to travel in this select company guarantees the continuation of greatness in our literature.

EDITORIAL NOTE

As background for reading this study, the reader should be aware of several editorial practices I have followed. To make clear Auden's practice at various times in his career, dates of initial book publication are supplied in parentheses after each first reference to an individual poem. Earlier magazine appearances are treated only where they are particularly enlightening. For all poems printed there, titles and texts are taken from *The Collected Poetry of W. H. Auden* (New York, 1945), cited in the notes as *CP*. Otherwise the texts are those of initial book publication. Revisions are noted only when they are particularly relevant.

A number of Auden's memorable critical writings are

now available in *The Dyer's Hand* (New York, 1962),
cited as *DH*. Quotations from his prose follow the form
of their original publication, but footnotes indicate appearances in *The Dyer's Hand* and any pertinent revisions.
This volume should not be confused with the essay bear-
ing the same title which appeared in *Anchor Review
No. 2* (1957).

CHAPTER I

THE ANTI-ROMANTIC MODERN

EVEN without knowing the author's name, any reasonably sensitive reader of a poem by W. H. Auden would speedily be aware that he was looking at a "modern" poem. Regardless of how traditional the stanza form might be, the tone, diction, and imagery work together to make a poem unmistakably post-Victorian. Take, for example, a recent nursery-rime limerick, "The Aesthetic Point of View" (1960):

> As the poets have mournfully sung,
> Death takes the innocent young,
>   The rolling-in-money,
>   The screamingly-funny,
> And those who are very well hung.[1]

The innocently conventional diction of the first lines gives way gradually through the colloquial feminine rimes of lines three and four to the jolt of obscene slang in the last line. The poem is apparently frivolous, hardly worthy of a "serious" poet; yet frivolousness is its essential point. Following Kierkegaard, the poem implicitly condemns the essential frivolity and amorality of the aesthetic point of view, which is concerned only with how interesting or striking a situation is.[2]

This little poem is instructive beyond its limited merit, for it reveals a tension central to Auden's mode, a tension between moral seriousness and the inescapable amorality

[1] *Homage to Clio* (New York, 1960), 74.
[2] For Auden's fuller explication of Kierkegaard on this point, see "A Preface to Kierkegaard," *The New Republic*, cx (May 15, 1944), 683-686.

of poetic artifice. The poem has a serious moral implication, but its admonition to those inclined to overvalue the aesthetic point of view is embedded in a form and style that do not even nod in the direction of serious moral contemplation. From the beginning Auden has wanted his skill in playing with words to stimulate efforts toward moral reform in his readers, but by the middle 1930's, when the basic terms of his characteristic mode had reached maturity, he was conscious of two crucial problems. First, he felt compelled to reject the direct communication of moral truth as a presumptuous assertion of his own will to power, analogous in politics to fascism. At the same time, his probing of the human psyche convinced him that direct preaching at an audience was simply ineffective. Highly self-conscious himself, he saw that modern readers would have to be trapped into self-awareness by indirect means. Since about 1935, then, most of his developments in manner and technique grow out of his search for more effective, though always indirect, didactic means. His philosophical position has changed over the years, but the root problems of writing a poem in his mode have not. In every poem he seeks a poetic strategy which can surprise, shock, or seduce his reader into serious self-examination, but simultaneously he seeks to avoid prejudging the terms in which the self-assessment should take place.

To state the tension another way, he must create a poetic mirror which is incisive, memorable, and inescapable, while insisting only that the reader should see in it his own deepest self. Paradoxically, one of Auden's difficulties in achieving this elusive end is his brilliance of technique. Each new poetic deftness, contrived to circumvent or cut through a reader's defenses, may allow him to be satisfied with himself for perceiving that brilliance. The poetic technique which makes didactic effectiveness possible may be just that instrument which defeats itself. Wrestling with this paradoxical aesthetic-moral problem has been Auden's major concern as a mature writer and an important stimulus to his inventiveness. The basic stances he has developed to deal with the problem constitute his poetic mode. In general orientation and method, the resulting poetry is clearly "modern." His poems are characteristically ironic and indirect, impersonal, and largely "anti-poetic."

Auden, of course, is not the innovator of these modern tendencies, as he himself is characteristically aware.[3] He is a second-generation modern who formed his conception of poetry as a disciple of T. S. Eliot and *The Criterion*.[4] During his Oxford years, starting in 1926, Auden appropriated the theories of Eliot which define the general outlines of the modern mode, and then went on to carry the same principles further than his master. For the purpose of describing Auden's particular version of the modern, we may divide Eliot's conception of poetry into three major areas of concern: (1) the relation of the poet to the body of existing poetry—the problem of tradition; (2) the relation of the poet as a man to his poem as an aesthetic artifact—the problem of personality; and (3) the relation of the poem to the audience—the problem of communication. Eliot's position in all three of these categories may be roughly described as "anti-Romantic" and as formulated in reaction against dominant literary notions

[3] "The Dyer's Hand," *The Anchor Review*, No. 2 (1957), 285-286.
[4] See "A Literary Transference," *Southern Review*, VI (Summer 1940), 80. Also *Letters from Iceland* (New York, 1937), 209.

of the nineteenth century. Eliot, and Auden after him, favors orientation to the poetic tradition over self-generated originality, self-contained poetic structure over personal catharsis, and conscious craftsmanship over inspiration. Nonetheless Auden has been far from a slavish follower of Eliot's theories and, as we shall see, the ways in which he has developed Eliot's ideas into his own distinctive contribution to modern poetry have led him even further into anti-Romanticism.

The relationship of "anti-Romanticism" to "Classicism" may require some clarification since the latter is the traditional term opposed to "Romanticism," no matter how the terms may be defined specifically. Classicism generally implies a world-view based on principles which happen to be opposed to those of Romanticism; its terms are usually derived from a larger "Classical" tradition. Anti-Romanticism, on the other hand, is self-consciously designed in reaction against Romanticism. Anti-Romanticism may share some attitudes and attributes with Classicism (as some of Auden's poetry resembles Dryden's), but it is distinguished by its motivation.

The anti-Romanticism of Eliot's concern for tradition is made clear early in "Tradition and the Individual Talent." He decries the tendency to praise a poet on the basis of "those aspects of his work in which he least resembles any one else."[5] Instead, Eliot proposes that both critic and poet become conscious of the relation of each new work to the existing order of works. The effect of Eliot's conception is to devalue the unique, subjective, and "original" qualities in poetry so valued by the Romantics; he substitutes a conscious concern for the artist's relation to poetic ancestors. Though "tradition" has not

[5] *Selected Essays* (New York, 1950), 4.

been such a conscious acquisition for Auden, and though he has adopted his own ancestors to sanction the kind of poetry he likes to write, both men share the basic desire to locate oneself by conscious relationship with earlier poetry.

Among the ancestors Auden has claimed and honored by imitation, some are Continental or American but most are English. With the exception of two major groups, his imagination moves freely over the entire scope of English poetry, appropriating whatever it finds useful. He can paraphrase the Anglo-Saxon "Battle of Maldon,"[6] or turn a meter of Tennyson's to a new use with equal facility.[7] He is equally adept at complex traditional forms like the sestina and simple fluid forms like the clerihew and the ballad. In addition, the knowledge of the poetic tradition exhibited in Auden's reviews and anthologies is imposing. In every case of close parallelism between an Auden poem and an earlier piece, he is almost certainly conscious of the precedent.

Two groups of English poets are conspicuously missing from the long list of those Auden has imitated or alluded to—the Metaphysicals and the Romantics. Metaphysical habits of imagination do appear in his work, but more noticeably in a general inclination toward "wit" than in direct imitation of particular forms or settings.[8] Auden may have deliberately turned his attention to pre-Elizabethan verse in order to avoid becoming dominated

[6] In "Which Side Am I Supposed to Be On?" *CP*, 138. See R. A. Long, "Auden's 'Ode to My Pupils,' " *Explicator*, VI (April 1948), Item 39.

[7] In "Get there if you can," *Poems* (London, 1930), 66-70. See also Henry W. Wells, *New Poets from Old* (New York, 1940), 68.

[8] See also Frederick P. W. MacDowell, " 'The Situation of Our Time': Auden in His American Phase," in *Aspects of American Poetry*, ed. Richard M. Ludwig (Columbus, Ohio, 1962), esp. 242.

[15]

by the models made fashionable through Eliot's sponsorship. He may also have been influenced toward medieval poetry by his Oxford tutor, Nevill Coghill, to whom he dedicated *The Dyer's Hand* in 1962. At the same time, Auden's later work has revealed such a strong native inclination toward moral allegory that he may have responded almost instinctively to poets like Langland.

Auden's studious avoidance of the Romantics is understandable since he is fond of developing his own views in explicit rejection of their ideas. Auden chose Shelley as his particular scapegoat and has torpedoed him in print periodically since 1934.[9] *Letters from Iceland* (1937) is shot through with criticism of the Wordsworthian attitude toward nature. Only Burns, Byron, and Blake does Auden recognize, and he chooses to imitate their satiric or light verse rather than their more serious poems.

Outside these two major groups, Auden's borrowing has been both wide and judicious. It is a tribute to his poetic integrity that he rarely allows his borrowing to do his work for him. Like Eliot he consistently makes a new poem out of the fragments he borrows. Eliot, however, especially in his earlier poems, usually employs quotations from the past for ironic contrast with the corrupted world of the present, whereas Auden habitually selects allusions which reinforce the dominant mood of his own poem. Auden's reader is less specifically dependent on his knowl-

---

[9] See, for example, "Psychology and Criticism," *New Verse*, No. 20 (April-May 1936), 22-24, Auden's review of Herbert Read, *In Defense of Shelley*. One of his stronger statements is: "How glad I am that the silliest remark ever made about poets, 'the unacknowledged legislators of the world,' was made by a poet whose work I detest. Sounds more like the secret police to me." "Squares and Oblongs," in *Poets at Work* (New York, 1948), 177. *DH*, 27, revised to be less directly personal.

edge of the original context of quotations or allusions, especially those whose source is in a foreign language.

Auden summarizes his attitudes toward the tradition as follows: "In poetry as in life, to lead one's own life means to relive the lives of one's parents and, through them, of all one's ancestors; the duty of the present is neither to copy nor to deny the past but to resurrect it."[10] In large measure he has succeeded in bringing about the rebirth of the past described in this mature statement. The poems in which he fails come mainly from his earliest writings when he was uncertain just who his true ancestors were and how he could successfully recreate them in poetry. Too often, for example, Auden's early imitations of Langland and his suppression of articles and connectives in the manner of a literal translation of Anglo-Saxon seem strained mannerisms. Similar devices used fifteen years later in *The Age of Anxiety* (1947) have a startling poetic evocativeness.

In "Tradition and the Individual Talent" Eliot pointed to the whole literature of Europe from Homer as the tradition the poet should have ready at hand. While Eliot's interests led him to concentrate on French and Italian writing, Auden's Icelandic family background influenced him to study Germanic literature. Christopher Isherwood reports that he was raised on the sagas, and certainly their influence on his early poems is marked.[11] In 1928 Auden went from Oxford to Germany and saw there the plays of Bertolt Brecht,[12] which were to be a

[10]"Yeats as an Example," *Kenyon Review*, x (Spring 1948), 188.
[11]"Some Notes on Auden's Early Poetry," *New Verse* (Auden Double Number), Nos. 26-27 (November 1937), 4. Reprinted in *Auden*, ed. Monroe K. Spears (Englewood Cliffs, New Jersey, 1964), 10. Mr. Auden verified this fact in a personal interview.
[12] See Eric Walter White, *Benjamin Britten*, rev. ed. (London, 1954), 21.

[17]

major influence on the dramas he wrote with Isherwood in the middle 1930's. Rilke became an important model for his use of the sonnet form and reinforced his own tendency to use physical objects as a projection of human qualities.[13] Like Eliot, Auden has more recently found inspiration in Dante, but his orientation continues to be primarily Germanic.

Further evidence of Auden's cosmopolitanism is found in "New Year Letter" (1941) where he hand-picks ancestors to be his poetic judges. Feeling that inescapably one must be judged, he selects these poets from those whom he admires most. Only four of the nine are English. They were not chosen for their direct influence on Auden; Langland, for example, is omitted and Catullus included. Rather, Auden selects poets who might sympathetically judge his efforts. As a result, these nine poets, together with Auden's reasons for choosing each one, define (at least as of 1941), the perspective in which he wishes his particular contribution to poetry to be seen. Dante is chief justice, flanked by Blake and Rimbaud. As he surveys the courtroom:

> There DRYDEN sits with modest smile,
> The master of the middle style,
> Conscious CATULLUS who made all
> His gutter-language musical,
> Black TENNYSON whose talents were
> For an articulate despair.[14]

Baudelaire is also watching, and Hardy and Rilke. Dante holds his position of chief judge by virtue of his cosmopolitan breadth of mind: "In concrete detail [he] saw

[13] W. H. Auden, "Rilke in English," *The New Republic*, C (September 6, 1939), 135-136.
[14] *CP*, 271.

the whole/ Environment that keeps the soul."[15] Similarly, Rimbaud is important not only for his strangling of an old rhetoric, but also for his awareness that "terror is not French."[16]

Besides the persistent concern for poetic ancestors, Eliot formulated for Auden other anti-Romantic attitudes as well. Most pervasive in Auden's poetic theory and practice is the impersonality enunciated by Eliot: "Poetry is not a turning loose of emotion, but an escape from emotion; it is not the expression of personality, but an escape from personality."[17] Stephen Spender reports Auden's view during the Oxford years in similar terms: "He told me that the subject of a poem was only the peg on which to hang the poetry. A poet was a kind of chemist who mixed his poems out of words, whilst remaining detached from his own feelings. Feelings and emotional experiences were only the occasion which precipitated into his mind the idea of a poem."[18] If Spender's memory is accurate, Auden was even thinking in a chemical metaphor for impersonality analogous to Eliot's in "Tradition and the Individual Talent."

Auden has continued to see the poet's task as impersonal; we have his continued delight in the impersonal "rules" of complex poetic forms to reinforce his numerous

[15] CP, 270. Auden's attempt to create an ecology of the soul is most prominent in later poems like "In Praise of Limestone" (1951), but it also plays an important part in earlier pieces like "In Memory of W. B. Yeats" (1940), where the topography of a city provides a metaphor for the progress of a soul.

[16] CP, 270. More recently Auden frankly describes himself as "a déraciné," and advocates a "beneficent anationality." See "A Dialogue with W. H. Auden," Hudson Review, III (Winter 1951), esp. 578 and 582.

[17] Selected Essays, 10.

[18] World Within a World (New York, 1951), 46.

extra-poetic statements. In 1954, for example, he succinctly reiterates his anti-Romantic bias. "Poetry demands
that the poet piously submit his precious personality to
impersonal limitations; he cannot say anything he likes
but only what they permit him to say."[19] An attempt to
evaluate such a poetry from a Romantic point of view is
bound to miss some elements that are essential to its
nature. Joseph Warren Beach is certainly on tenuous
ground when he suggests that "In Memory of W. B.
Yeats" and "September 1, 1939" are, among others, "earnest, direct, and manly" expressions of the poet's personal
feelings.[20] In none of his poems can one feel sure that
the speaker is Auden himself. In the course of his career
he has demonstrated impressive facility in speaking
through any sort of dramatic persona; accordingly, the
choice of an intimate, personal tone does not imply the
direct self-expression of the poet. It is precisely self-control
and rationality that lead Auden to choose Dante as his
chief judge. He can hope for sympathetic understanding
from the Dante who, out of "Amor Rationalis," sees that
men he personally likes may require a place in the In-
ferno. Heaven, says Auden, may be "full of people you
don't like."[21] When a poet like Auden embraces restraint
of his personal impulses as a means to his art, a Romantic
reading, attuned to the expression of personality, may
miss the poem's essential character as supra-personal performance.

Auden's response to the problems of tradition and personality should demonstrate the kind of consistency that

[19] "The Pool of Narcissus," New Yorker, xxx (December 18,
1954), 144.
[20] Auden Canon, 247.
[21] "Conversation on Cornelia Street, V: A Dialogue with W. H.
Auden (with Howard Griffin)," Accent, xiii (Winter 1953), 46.

constitutes his characteristic mode. While he adopted different poetic ancestors as his ideas changed, he has never worked for long outside the context of some poetic precedent. He sometimes, especially during his first decade of writing, adopted an intimate or confessional tone, but the perspective of his whole work reveals this voice as only one of many through which he can dramatize his views. Similarly, the impersonal relation of poet to poem is evident in his progressive tendency through the 1930's and 1940's to submit his impulses to the rational control implicit in allegory. Auden's poetry, as much as that of any Romantic, is the product of a unique encounter with the world, but, unlike the Romantic, he does not ask acceptance of his vision because it is unique or because it is his.

A related opposition to Romanticism centers around the third major problem for Auden as modern poet—the search for an audience. Where the Romantic emphasizes self-expression, Auden seeks communication. As he put it in 1936, "Those who have no interest in communication do not become artists either; they become mystics or madmen."[22] But one must be able to locate an audience to communicate anything successfully, and this problem was a crucial one for Auden for many years. Characteristically he is aware and perhaps even hyperconscious of his audience. Many of his changes in style and manner have been stimulated by the attempt to isolate and engage different sorts of audiences. The problem has been less acute since 1940 and his projected audience has changed relatively little. Though he may have wanted a more popular audience, he has settled most often for the

[22] "Introduction," *The Oxford Book of Light Verse* (London, 1938), vii.

[21]

educated and somewhat sophisticated literary public—say, readers of the *New Yorker*. His frequent reliance on American slang may limit some of his more recent poems to readers on this side of the Atlantic, just as the English schoolboy slang in his poems of the early 1930's handicaps the non-British audience. Still, he is clearly aiming at an urban and urbane reader who will respond to the expression of moral seriousness through deft and witty verbal play.

During the last half of the 1930's, however, Auden's postulated audience was somewhat different. He sought a relatively unsophisticated "proletarian" audience. With characteristically easy transition from politics to poetry Auden remarks: "The social virtues of a real democracy are brotherhood and intelligence, and the parallel linguistic virtues are strength and clarity."[23] The result in Auden's poetry was a startling change toward transparency in meaning and conventional rimed stanzas in form.

It has been dangerously easy to attribute these poetic changes in the middle 1930's to a conversion to communism. Indeed, Auden encouraged such interpretations of his newly acquired techniques by speaking of poetry in political terms, by publishing in the left press in England, and by accepting Marxist analyses of social phenomena in his extra-poetic statements.[24] The influence of Marxism on his poetry should not, however, be overemphasized. Auden himself recognized his inability to reach a truly proletarian audience. "Personally, the kind of poetry I should like to write but can't is 'the thoughts of a wise

[23] "The Public vs. the Late Mr. William Butler Yeats," *Partisan Review*, VI (Spring 1939), 51.

[24] See, for example, Auden's contribution to *I Believe*, ed. Clifton Fadiman (New York, 1939), 3-16.

man in the speech of the common people.' "[25] The audience he could and did reach in the late 1930's was that
of the educated middle class with left-wing or revolutionary sympathies.[26] However, the simple concern for changing the status quo or even opposition to fascism in Germany and Spain do not make one a Communist. Stephen
Spender's comments are worth noting because of his close
contact with Auden in this period: "He had a firmer grip
of Marxist ideology, and more capacity to put this into
good verse than many writers who were closer to Communism. This led to the legend that he went through a
Communist phase. But his poem, 'A Communist to
Others,' is an exercise in entering a point of view not his
own. It is his summing up of conversations with Commu-
nists rather like the ones I used to have with Chalmers
in Berlin."[27] Marxism was only indirectly an influence on
Auden's poetry. It did indicate a relatively well-defined
audience to whom or through whom Auden felt he could
make his private vision public.

[25] "Poets, Poetry, and Taste," *The Highway*, xxix (December
1936), 44. This periodical itself was published by the Workers'
Educational Association.
[26] David Daiches over twenty years ago, in *Poetry and the Modern World* (Chicago, 1940), pointed out that the major problem
of Auden's first decade of publishing was to find the right sort of
public to or through which he could make public his private vision.
Mr. Daiches defines the postulated public of *Look, Stranger* (1936;
American title, *On This Island*) as the ideal schoolboy (p. 228).
Indeed, this volume is the first one in which the tone of the author
seems certain and the reader does not worry about which side he
is supposed to be on. By postulating the ideal schoolboy as audience, Auden could articulate his criticisms of contemporary events
and people to a fairly well-defined group—all those who, like the
schoolboy, are not content with the state of affairs as they presently are, those with revolutionary tendencies.
[27] *World Within a World*, 225. Auden chose not to reprint "A
Communist to Others" after its appearance as poem xiv in *On This
Island* (New York, 1937) and *Look, Stranger* (London, 1936).

[23]

There are also some purely aesthetic factors influencing the new-found transparency of Auden's poetry in this period. In the middle 1930's he began to rely more than ever before on anti-Romantic impersonality in organizing his poems. In 1935 he met Benjamin Britten[28] and began writing songs and ballads, the words for music which were to culminate in the libretto for Stravinsky's opera, *The Rake's Progress* (1951). Songs require relatively simple and easily grasped imagery and in that sense can appeal to a wider reading public. They are also, in Auden's conception, of all kinds of poetry "the least personal and most verbal."[29] A further commitment to impersonality is evident in Auden's new interest in light verse. He edited *The Oxford Book of Light Verse* in 1936 and began to produce his own *vers de société*. In Auden's hands, light verse, as in "The Aesthetic Point of View" quoted at the beginning of this chapter, becomes a sharp, impersonal instrument which attacks the self-deception of men, poets or not, who believe they can be "seriously" sincere:

> I will content myself with asserting dogmatically that, this season, the man of good will will wear his heart up his sleeve, not on it. For better or worse, we who live in this age not only feel but are critically conscious of our emotions . . . and, in consequence, again for better or worse, a naïve rhetoric, one that is not confessedly "theatrical," is now impossible in poetry. The honest manly style is today only suited to Iago.[30]

[28] White, *Benjamin Britten*, 22.
[29] "Foreword" to William Dickey, *Of the Festivity* (New Haven, 1959), xi.
[30] "Introduction" to John Betjeman, *Slick But Not Streamlined* (Garden City, 1947), 15.

Before 1935 or so, Auden was still in the process of working out the lineaments of the mode which has become characteristically his, but in the perspective of his work as a whole his anti-Romantic leanings are clear. His initial strategy to avoid the "honest manly style" was primarily to cloak his poems in obscurity. Eliot had predicted that modern poetry must be "difficult"; Auden, from 1926 till roughly 1935, seemed sometimes to take Eliot at his word and to manufacture obscurity so that he could be "modern." It is easy to share the exasperation of Malcolm Cowley in 1934 when he concluded: "His principal fault, I think, is his damnable and perverse obscurity."[31] There are two essential types of obscurity in Auden's early verse. First is obscurity created by his manipulation of language, especially syntax and occasionally diction; second is obscurity resulting from the small, self-contained audience Auden felt he could write for.

Syntactical obscurity results most commonly from the suppression of connectives or the indefinite reference of pronouns. Syntactical short-cuts and a parallel suppression of the full context of poetic statements lead to confused symbolism in a number of poems. Take the following stanza, first published in 1930, for example:

> A neutralizing peace
> And an average disgrace
> Are honour to discover
> For later other.[32]

The sense of the stanza is reasonably clear; it can be paraphrased as follows: it is a worthwhile achievement for

[31] "Spender and Auden," *The New Republic*, LXXX (September 26, 1934), 190.
[32] "The Questioner Who Sits So Sly," *CP*, 179. The poem's title, added in 1945, comes from Blake's "Auguries of Innocence."

your descendants to remember if you manage to accomplish even a limited goal, not victory but "a neutralizing peace." In the context of the entire poem, however, the stanza fails to make sense because the poem sets up no oppositions that could be resolved in "a neutralizing peace." All the preceding stanzas offer for the brave is defeat by the enemy and disgrace at home. If there is a context in which this frustration could be considered a "neutralizing peace," the suppression of that frame of reference makes the symbolism impenetrably obscure.

Auden's interest in the clipped, disconnected style has two important motivations. First is simply a demand for attention by startling phraseology. Second, and more important, is the impulse described by Richard Hoggart: "It is the verse of a young man prepared to experiment widely with forms and manners of expression, but particularly suspicious of lushness, and anxious to evolve a hard, cerebral style."[33] The anti-Romantic starkness of expression is the more startling because so many of the themes of these early poems reveal attitudes traditionally associated with Romanticism. There is nostalgia for childhood, yearning for a trust in the unconscious and the flesh after D. H. Lawrence and Blake,[34] and a considerable measure of trust in the perfectibility of man. This incongruity of theme and poetic expression illustrates the complexity of Auden's growth. Not until near 1940 did his themes become as consistently anti-Romantic as his mode of presenting them. In fact, starting from the initial impact of Eliot, Auden's progressively greater anti-Roman-

[33] *Auden, An Introductory Essay* (London, 1951), 19.
[34] See esp. *Poems* (London, 1930). See also lengthy discussion of these subjects in the unpublished dissertation (Northwestern, 1958) by Hugh Alan Nelson, "Individuals of a Group: The Nineteen-Thirties Poetry of W. H. Auden, C. Day Lewis, and Stephen Spender," esp. 100ff.

ticism may well reflect a more or less conscious revolt against Romantic impulses he found within himself.[35]

The second major source of obscurity in this earliest period is the small audience that Auden felt he could reach. Again and again in his analyses of the problems of the modern poet, Auden laments the lack of a homogeneous society with shared beliefs or at least shared images and symbols that a poet could draw on. In 1936 he put it thus: "The problem of the modern poet, as for everyone else to-day, is how to find or form a genuine community, in which each has his valued place and can feel at home."[36] There was only one place in the England of 1930 where Auden could feel at home and that was in the group of his college friends, including, most prominently, Stephen Spender, C. Day Lewis, Christopher Isherwood, Rex Warner, and Edward Upward.[37] Understandably, Auden concludes that amusing one's friends is a primary motivation for an artist:

> Art, if it doesn't start there, at least ends,
> Whether aesthetics like the thought or not,
> In an attempt to entertain our friends;
> And our first problem is to realise what
> Peculiar friends the modern artist's got; . . .[38]

[35] See fuller discussion of Romanticism in Auden's early verse in Chapter 3. A work as probing as *The Enchafèd Flood: A Romantic Iconography of the Sea* (New York, 1950, and London, 1951) indicates that Auden understands very well the Romanticism he so forcibly rejects.

[36] *Oxford Light Verse*, xix.

[37] See valuable discussion of mutual influence and common symbolism in the writings of members of this informal group in the unpublished dissertation (Wisconsin, 1956) by Justin Maynard Replogle, "The Auden Group: The Nineteen-Thirties Poetry of W. H. Auden, C. Day Lewis, and Stephen Spender."

[38] "Letter to Lord Byron," *Letters from Iceland* (New York, 1937), 103.

The particular friends that Auden had were witty, intelligent, and highly educated; they were acquainted with all the latest theories, especially in psychology. The obscurity that results from writing for the coterie appears in private allusions and esoteric theorizing. However opaque some of these poems seem to a reader from outside the group, it seems probable that the poems do have intelligible meaning. Stephen Spender insists that: "Every line of his poetry—which has been called obscure—*means* something in the sense that it has an immediate relation to some real event which he interprets as a psychological or spiritual or sociological symptom."[39] If Spender is right, then presumably one could understand presently opaque images if he knew either the real events or the theoretical systems for isolating symptoms. Auden himself criticizes obscurity in a way that suggests he would not consciously indulge in it. "One must begin by distinguishing between riddle, which is, I believe, a fundamental element in poetry, and obscurity, which is an aesthetic vice." The difference, he suggests, is obvious to the crossword puzzle addict, who responds to an answer with either "What a fool I was. Of course that's it," or "The clue was unfair. Four or five other words would fit it equally well."[40] Those poems that an outsider can decipher suggest that most of the "obscure" poems are not intrinsically so. However, they can be criticized for failing to make their vision available to more than a handful of people.

There is one further sort of obscurity in the early poetry which is better understood as an imitation of Eliot than

[39] "W. H. Auden and His Poetry," *Atlantic*, cxcii (July 1953), 77. Reprinted in *Auden*, ed. Monroe K. Spears, 34.
[40] "A Contemporary Epic," *Encounter*, ii (February 1954), 68.

as a practice peculiar to Auden. A number of early poems, including Auden's most ambitious early work, *The Orators* (1932), are constructed with a "logic of the imagination" as opposed to a "logic of concepts."[41] These Auden poems are obscure in the manner of "The Waste Land"; like it they attempt "to find the verbal equivalent for states of mind and feeling" by presenting a succession of images without explicit conceptual relation.

The Orators is only partially successful[42] and Auden soon thereafter abandoned the associational logic of a succession of images. He became interested less in simply defining the state of the world and more in expressing a thesis as to what should be done. As a result, Auden after the early 1930's characteristically uses images to illustrate a diagnosis of the contemporary situation. Thus he puts images to a more clearly conceptual use in a typical poem of the late 1930's, "Dover 1937":

> Steep roads, a tunnel through the downs are the
>   approaches;
> A ruined pharos overlooks a constructed bay;
> The sea-front is almost elegant; all this show
> Has, somewhere inland, a vague and dirty root:
>   Nothing is made in this town.[43]

The poet's interest here is in defining and communicating a conceptualized insight into the contemporary malaise with all its uncreative passivity and triviality. As time has

[41] T. S. Eliot, "Introduction" to St.-John Perse, *Anabasis*, 2nd rev. ed. (New York, 1949), 10.

[42] See analysis in Chapter 3 of one excerpt from *The Orators* entitled "Have a Good Time." Monroe Spears's analysis of the whole work is by far the best in print. See *The Poetry of W. H. Auden*, 45-58. The mature Auden judges the poem as a "fair notion fatally injured," *CP*, Preface [vii].

[43] *CP*, 111.

passed, Auden has tended to make his themes even more conceptually clear; "New Year Letter" (1941), for example, is virtually rational discourse in verse after the manner of Dryden. In general, one may say that Auden's movement away from Eliot's mode of associational organization represents a more complete commitment to anti-Romanticism than Eliot himself made. Another indication is Auden's frequent choice of allegory with its associated control of emotive faculties by rationality. Bringing what one accepts or rejects to full consciousness is Auden's mature ideal for both artist and man.[44]

As Auden reintroduced the logic and the language of concepts into his poetry, he left behind an important part of the conception of poetry suggested by Eliot and developed by important contemporary critics like Cleanth Brooks and Kenneth Burke. Since their conception of poetry has been powerful in the criticism of recent years, it may help to define his mode if we examine interchanges between Auden and these critics. Perhaps his deviation from their conception has encouraged the grudging acceptance accorded most of his volumes since 1939. Cleanth Brooks in *Modern Poetry and the Tradition*[45] complimented Auden's work to that date; despite some strictures, Auden's response, as expressed in his review, was basically sympathetic.[46] But with the fuller development of this poetic theory Auden could not entirely agree. In 1949 Brooks summarized his conception in an article entitled, "Irony as a Principle of Structure": "One can sum up modern poetic technique by calling it the rediscovery of

[44] See "For the Time Being" (1944), *CP*, 451.
[45] (Chapel Hill, 1939), 126 ff. Reprinted in *Auden*, ed. Monroe K. Spears, 15-25.
[46] "Against Romanticism," *The New Republic*, CII (February 5, 1940), 187.

[30]

metaphor and the full commitment to metaphor. The poet can legitimately step out into the universal only by first going through the narrow door of the particular. The poet does not select an abstract theme and then embellish it with concrete details. . . . Through his metaphors, he risks saying it partially and obscurely, and risks not saying it at all. But the risk must be taken, for direct statement leads to abstraction and threatens to take us out of poetry altogether."[47] Here is defined in general terms a frequent criticism made of Auden's work since 1940. Insofar as he made one, Auden's reply is contained in reviews he wrote in the early 1940's. He notes that Kenneth Burke's *Philosophy of Literary Form* is essentially literary apologetics for a society hostile to poetry. Such criticism, to Auden, merely keeps up the faithful; it does not convert the heathen. As far as the theory itself is concerned, he protests that concentrating on the symbolic meaning of "This-House-plus" has the effect of making ambiguities per se the whole source of poetic interest and ignores the general meaning which can be "not-This-House-but-all-possible-houses."[48] Against Burke's valuing of ambiguity and symbolic suggestiveness, Auden asserts his own anti-Romantic concern for the abstract and general expressed with strength and clarity. Auden does not seem to feel he is "out of poetry altogether," but insofar as modern criticism has had difficulty in dealing with abstract poetry like that of Dryden, it has had limited openness to the mature Auden.

There are still, of course, many similarities between Auden's characteristic mode and the Eliot-Brooks con-

---

[47] First published in *Literary Opinion in America*, ed. Morton Dauwen Zabel, rev. ed. (New York, 1951), 729.

[48] "A Grammar of Assent," *The New Republic*, cv (July 14, 1941), 59.

ception of poetry. Auden's tendency to write dramatized poetry including more than one "character" or point of view fulfills Brooks's notion that a poem should project tension between opposing ideas. Brooks wants all poetic statements to be read as if they were speeches in a drama; Auden's poems, with their consistent use of a persona or mask to express ideas indirectly, encourage such a reading. Also, both Auden and Brooks agree that, contrary to Romantic critical opinion, wit and fancy have as much place in poetry as imagination, and intellect as much as emotion. However, from a position of basic agreement with these New Critical conceptions, Auden has gone on to advance ideas which would be unacceptable to most followers of Eliot and Brooks.[49] For instance, Auden's mature view that an essential element in poetry is "the poetic ornamentation of simple questions and answers by casting them in the form of riddles"[50] comes close to the neo-Classical conception of metaphor as the decoration of thought, too close, perhaps, to be entirely congenial to one with an unqualified commitment to metaphor as primary vehicle for poetry. The same, as we have seen, applies to Auden's tendency to deal directly in his poems with the abstract and general by means of allegory.

As final measure of the distance Auden has departed from the Eliot-Brooks conception of poetry, we may call on one of Auden's infrequent printed comments on Eliot.

---

[49] It seems clear by now that the "New Critics," despite many protestations to the contrary, perpetuate a number of Romantic preferences. See Murray Krieger, *The New Apologists for Poetry* (Minneapolis, 1956), esp. 123-139 re Brooks; Frank Kermode, *Romantic Image* (London, 1957); Richard Foster, *The New Romantics* (Bloomington, Indiana, 1962).

[50] "Introduction" to *The Portable Greek Reader* (New York, 1948), 5. See also "A Contemporary Epic," *Encounter*, II (February 1954), 69.

Reviewing a volume of Kipling's verse edited and introduced by Eliot, Auden says:

> In his essay, Mr. Eliot draws a distinction between
> poetry and verse:
>
> > 'For other poets—at least, for some other poets—the
> > poem may begin to shape itself in fragments of musi-
> > cal rhythm, and its structure will first appear in terms
> > of something analogous to musical form. . . . What
> > fundamentally distinguishes his [Kipling's] "verse"
> > from "poetry" is the subordination of musical inter-
> > est. . . . There is a harmonics of poetry which is not
> > merely beyond the range of the poems—it would
> > interfere with the intention.'
>
> This distinction is real and neatly describes the dif-
> ference between the kind of poetry written by Eliot
> and the kind written by Kipling, but, so defined, there
> are more verse or ballad writers and fewer poets, I think,
> than Mr. Eliot seems to imply. Ben Jonson, for in-
> stance, who wrote out a prose draft which he then versi-
> fied, Dunbar, Butler's "Hudibras," most of Burns, By-
> ron's "Don Juan," etc.[51]

This distinction equally well describes the difference
between the kinds of poetry written by Auden and Eliot.
It is worth noting that Auden, at one time or another,
has honored most of the poets in his list of "versifiers"
by direct imitation or parody.

This final quality of Auden's work—his tendency to
write "verse" rather than "poetry" as they are usually defined in this century—has carried his anti-Romanticism

[51] "The Poet of the Encirclement," *The New Republic*, CIX
(October 25, 1943), 579. Auden's ellipses in quotation from Eliot.

beyond the point where standard modern criticism can deal with his poetry comfortably. To grant Auden the acclaim he deserves would appear to open the door into poetry for "prose" thinking. Yet to understand and appreciate what he has been doing over the years, we must first isolate his characteristic mode of poetry without indulging our preconceptions of what it ought to be. In 1964 Auden succinctly reiterates what *his* aim has been: "The ideal at which I aim is a style which shall combine the drab, sober truthfulness of prose with a poetic uniqueness of expression."[52] Just how Auden could come to state his goal in terms such as these is the subject for investigation next.

[52] "Reply," in "A Symposium on W. H. Auden's 'A Change of Air,'" *Kenyon Review*, xxvi (Winter 1964), 207. Reprinted in *The Contemporary Poet as Artist and Critic*, ed. Anthony Ostroff (Boston, 1964), 186.

CHAPTER II

THE POETICS OF PARABLE

"GENUINELY didactic by nature, he is one of the outstanding teachers of his time." Thus in personal terms, Stephen Spender describes the dominant intention behind Auden's poetry. The didactic poet, like every teacher, hopes that those who encounter his work will learn something. To justify the particular way his poems attempt to induce learning, Auden has developed over the years his own brand of anti-Romantic poetics. Spender goes on to recount an anecdote which deserves repeating for the accuracy with which it portrays Auden's understanding of poetic teaching:

"On another occasion he made a criticism which, while completely justified, emphasized the difference between us: 'I suggest that you attach too much importance to your emotions.' One day, when he had argued more seriously than usual to this effect, I remarked that he was only saying what I had come to think myself. 'I agree with you,' I said, 'and I shall try to change.' At this he buried his head in his hands and exclaimed: 'But don't you realize that I don't want you to change? Why do you take me seriously? I thought you were one of the few people who wouldn't do so. What's so awful in this country [America] is that people will take one seriously. . . .'

"The point of his complaint becomes clear, I think, if one substitutes the word 'literally' for 'seriously.' He wanted me to see the point of entering into intellectual attitudes not temperamentally my own. He did not wish me to abandon what was intrinsic to me. To take him seriously in being persuaded that I could or should really change was both to take him too literally and not seriously enough."[1]

Similarly, in his poetry Auden hopes to involve the reader in a self-critical dialogue with the new perspective on himself and his world that is presented in the poem. But achieving this end is more difficult as a poet than as a man, because the poet does not have a specified audience. Auden is driven to a special kind of generality—his poem must be able to lead a variety of readers to respond, each according to his own life situation. The poem must act as a kind of parable, not as a sermon. If its terms are too abstract, no one may be moved to self-examination; if they are too specific, the range of readers who will be reached may be painfully narrow. Avoiding these two extremes presents a perpetual challenge for poetry, to balance the claims of what Sir Philip Sidney long ago termed philosophy and history. Auden has developed a special form of allegory to handle this problem, which we shall examine in its place; what is important in the present context is the poetics in which Auden has evolved his conception of restricted didactics. For one who has often repeated his scorn for systematic poetic theories, Auden has exhibited, at least since 1935, a remarkable consistency in formulating the basic tenets of his poetics.

At the outset we can observe that Auden's didactic poetic is anti-Romantic in its conception. In place of the primary Romantic uses of poetry for self-expression or celebration of the poet's sensibility, he substitutes a dominant concern for what the poem can accomplish for the audi-

[1] *World Within a World*, 270-272.

ence. If autobiographical details are present in the poem, their origins will be irrelevant. Auden asks acceptance of his vision not because it is unique or because it is his, but because the reader, he hopes, will feel compelled to recognize its relevance to his personal existence. The poem, in other words, becomes a performance for the sake of the audience.

As Spender's anecdote suggests, Auden sees each man as independently responsible for evaluating every suggestion of what he should be or become. What the teacher and the poet do is to offer fresh perspectives which are worthy of a place in an individual's critical self-examination. To take the poem literally is to twist it into a command or a moral imperative. Yet the self Auden, or any man, puts forward to the world is necessarily a role-playing or posed self, not an honest self-revelation. Man is in the position of a professional actor who finds it difficult to catch himself off stage and out of costume to see what he is "really" like. The human individual cannot perform an action which is out of the line of vision of his own self-consciousness. Hence, to Auden the moralist, neither poet nor reader ought to take his own performances literally (in Spender's sense). In fact, the overly literal acceptance of their own role-playing selves is one of the major characteristics Auden condemns in Romantics of all kinds—witness the title of a course he taught at Swarthmore in the early 1940's: *Romanticism from Rousseau to Hitler.*[2] Even more important, the proper understanding of one's role-playing self is crucial in any effort toward moral reform. As the commentary in *The Age of Anxiety* puts it: "Human beings are, necessarily, actors who cannot become something before they have

[2] See Spears, *Poetry of Auden*, 248.

[37]

first pretended to be it; and they can be divided, not into the hypocritical and the sincere, but into the sane who know they are acting and the mad who do not."[3] The poetry appropriate to this view of humanity will predictably be "insincere" and theatrical; the accompanying poetics will conceive the poem as performance for the spectator, because through his self-conscious ego the maker is himself partially a spectator.

When as an Oxford undergraduate he began laying the groundwork of his didactic poetics, Auden insisted first on the limited participation of the poet's personality in the poem. As Spender reports some of his primary assertions:

> A poet must have no opinions, no decided views which he seeks to put across in his poetry.
>
> Above all, poetry must in no way be concerned with politics.
>
> A poet must be clinical, dispassionate about life. The poet feels much less strongly about things than do other people.[4]

This impersonality in the relation of poet to his work, however, is simply one side of the coin as Auden was soon to see. The suppression of the poet's personality focuses attention on the function of the poem for its reader. On the basis of his thoughtful response to Freud, Auden in 1935 described that function as moral and therapeutic:

> The task of psychology, or art for that matter, is not to tell people how to behave, but by drawing their atten-

---

[3] *The Age of Anxiety* (New York, 1947), 109.
[4] "Auden and His Poetry," 74. Reprinted in *Auden*, ed. Monroe K. Spears, 27.

tion to what the impersonal unconscious is trying to tell them, and by increasing their knowledge of good and evil, to render them better able to choose, to become increasingly morally responsible for their destiny.[5]

Over the years Auden has continued to praise Freud for his insistence that the goal of therapy is to make the patient better able to handle his personal choices.[6] In the same article Auden goes on to describe the kind of poetry that can accomplish this function, for the first time characterizing the poem as parable:

> You cannot tell people what to do, you can only tell them parables; and that is what art really is, particular stories of particular people and experiences, from which each according to his immediate and peculiar needs may draw his own conclusions.[7]

Auden's conclusions at this point may well reflect his observation that sermonizing is simply ineffective in influencing readers to be more moral. We may also note, however, that his position conveniently frees the poet from responsibility for any moral commitments which his own uncertainties about the world might make embarrassing. If he sanctions *any* use of the poem that the reader may desire or need, the poet will certainly avoid propagandistic self-assertion, but he may go too far towards moral relativism. In any case Auden clearly rejects the use of art as a literal guidebook for travel through life.

Since 1941 Auden has been particularly vehement in

[5] "Art and Psychology," in *The Arts Today*, ed. G. Grigson (London, 1935), 18.
[6] See, for one instance, "Sigmund Freud," *The New Republic*, cxxvii (October 6, 1952), 16-17. Auden's mode clearly has important analogies to non-directive therapy.
[7] "Art and Psychology," 18-19.

his insistence on the separation of art and life. As he puts it in "New Year Letter," "Art is not life and cannot be/ A midwife to society."[8] He finds any assertion that art has literal moral value a symptom of the Romantic disease he is concerned to combat:

> The romantic movement has been, *au fond*, an attempt to find a new nonsupernatural Catholicism, and because art is a shared thing and so in this sense Catholic, one of the romantic symptoms has been an enormous exaggeration of the importance of art as a guide to life, and, within art itself, an emphasis on the unconscious, the childish, and the irrational in the hope that in these lie human unity.[9]

In his self-conscious anti-Romanticism Auden goes out of his way to remind his reader that the human insights expressed in a poem require conscious assessment, not unthinking application. His poems advertise their own limited value as guides to conduct. Another of Auden's metaphorical descriptions of the relation of art to life may reinforce this point. To counter the Romantic confusion of art with life, he suggests that "art *has* life . . . human experience transmuted into its own unique being as a tree transmutes water and sunlight." In the reader's personal encounter with art, the poem "doesn't give information but a revelation of itself which is simultaneously a revelation of ourselves."[10]

At the same time that he dissociates himself from what he would call a Romantic presumptuousness on the part

[8] *CP*, 267.
[9] "Mimesis and Allegory," *English Institute Annual*, 1940, ed. Rudolf Kirk (New York, 1941), 17.
[10] "Verismo Opera," in George R. Marek, ed., *The World Treasury of Grand Opera* (New York, 1957), 148. *DH*, 482.

of the artist, Auden can, in another mood, express irritation at the fact that art does not have more impact on life: "The frivolity of art is that it cannot have much effect in changing people. No matter how utterly convincing, didactic art cannot succeed in changing society. . . . The best definition of man is the ungrateful biped."[11] Such annoyance at the necessity he sees for a restrained sort of didacticism suggests that Auden developed his parable poetics at least in part as self-admonition, as a corrective to a tendency in himself to overvalue words as a substitute for deeds. Most poets, after all, are content to send their poems into print, assuming as a matter of course that readers will do with them as they will. Auden is remarkable in the degree to which he self-consciously attempts to predict and preclude unthinking responses by his reader. Inevitably we suspect that Auden's repeated emphasis on the limited effectiveness of poetry is partly directed at himself. As we shall see in relation to Auden's allegory, the Romantic impulses expressed in his earliest poetry tend to support this tentative conclusion.

In 1948 Auden made what is probably his best known statement of parable poetics, still conceiving the poem as a tool of self-knowledge for both poet and reader:

> Two theories of poetry. Poetry as a magical means for inducing desirable emotions and repelling undesirable emotions in oneself and others, or Poetry as a game of knowledge, a bringing to consciousness, by naming them, of emotions and their hidden relationships.

[11] "A Dialogue with W. H. Auden (with Howard Griffin)," *Hudson Review*, III (Winter 1951), 578-579. The final quip is borrowed from Dostoevsky's *Notes from Underground*; see *White Nights and Other Stories*, tr. Constance Garnett (New York, 1918), 72.

The first view was held by the Greeks, and is now held by MGM, Agit-Prop, and the collective public of the world. They are wrong.[12]

Auden rejects the "magical" use of poetry as propaganda for any system of values, no matter how desirable, because to him as to the great moralists of all generations in the West there is a significant moral difference between doing good like a puppet, and *choosing* to do good.[13] Describing poetry as a *game* of knowledge emphasizes the limited impact of art on moral choice. Poetry like all games, indeed like all knowledge, is essentially frivolous, "because it does not of itself move what is serious, the will. Only the will can will to make use of knowledge."[14] His conception now, however, is more sharply defined than in 1935. Instead of leaving the reader free to make any use of the poem he may desire, Auden now wants him to become conscious of "emotions and their hidden relationships."

Through the 1950's to the present, Auden's poetics have continued to evolve, though the degree of reorientation in his views is not yet certain. It is clear that the inaugural lecture of Auden's term as Oxford Professor of Poetry in 1956 announces a new conception of the *genesis* of poetry and its personal function for the maker. Instead of bringing hidden emotional relationships to consciousness by naming them, the poem, by naming, pays homage to the existence of sacred beings or events.[15] Possibly, after at least twenty years of conscious effort

[12] "Squares and Oblongs," 173. "Agit-Prop" is a contraction of "Agitation and Propaganda Bureau," a part of the organization of most national Communist parties.

[13] See, for example, "The Dyer's Hand," 298-299.

[14] "Squares and Oblongs," 170.

[15] *Making, Knowing, and Judging,* 30. DH, 57.

devoted to knowing himself, exploring the personal and cultural unconscious, Auden now finds himself relatively predictable. Hence, perhaps, he finds that he is moved to poetry by what seems a different impulse. When he re-reads existing poetry, he often encounters this same poetic response to the numinous:

> How many poems have been written . . . upon one of these three themes:
> This was sacred but now it is profane. Alas, or thank goodness!
> This is sacred but ought it to be?
> This is sacred but is that so important?
> But it is from the sacred encounters of his imagination that a poet's impulse to write a poem arises. Thanks to [the] language he need not name them directly unless he wishes; . . . Some poems are directly *about* the sacred beings they were written *for*: others are not, and in that case no reader can tell what was the original encounter which provided the impulse for the poem.[16]

It is important that the poet's sacred encounter is essentially private; the reader will know of it only what the poet chooses to reveal. The poem can still function publicly as didactic parable.

In 1964, discussing his recent poem "A Change of Air," Auden suggests how his differing perspectives can be synthesized. He describes the genesis of this poem while he was working on the translation of Goethe's *Italienische Reise*. He was fascinated by the contrast between inner and outer biography implicit in Goethe's sudden departure from his accustomed habits to go to Italy under

[16] *Ibid.*, 32. *DH*, 59, adds the [the] and has minor variations in punctuation.

an assumed name. But the origin is hidden in the resulting poem, which Auden openly describes as a parable: "I set out, therefore, to try to write a poem in which it would be impossible for a reader to be distracted from its personal relevance to himself by thinking of Goethe or, even more mistakenly, of me."[17]

In the last twenty years Auden has become more publicly insistent on a basic dichotomy in terms of which every reader needs to examine himself. "A Change of Air,"[18] for example, directs his attention to the relation between his ego and the personae he adopts both at home and elsewhere. In more general terms Auden's reader is asked to be aware of his present state of being and the future being he is in the process of becoming. In 1953 he put it thus: "Each person, I believe, has two faces— that given him and the one he is trying to become; through will he can work on the first to achieve the second."[19] He clearly implies that the reader must critically evaluate the state of his two faces, though the poet will not attempt to predetermine what the conclusion should be. Auden is like a broad-minded prophet who insists forcefully on the need for a religious perspective on life, but offers no creed to structure that perspective. To him the faces of being and becoming are essential terms of human existence and every man needs to be conscious of what he is willing to become.

This short survey of Auden's changing statements over the years has shown him sharpening and enriching his conception of poetry without ever discarding the core of didactic poetics. There are, as has been implied, points

[17] "Symposium," *Kenyon Review*, XXVI (Winter 1964), 205. Reprinted in *The Contemporary Poet*, ed. Anthony Ostroff, 184.

[18] First published in *Encounter*, XVIII (January 1962), 93.

[19] "A Dialogue with W. H. Auden (with Howard Griffin)," *Partisan Review*, XX (January 1953), 81.

of discernible development since his initial articulation of the poetics of parable in 1935. By the time of "New Year Letter" in 1941, his mature view of man as actor is fully developed. By 1948 he is more certain that poems should help readers establish more conscious contact with their inner emotional selves. In 1956 he distinguishes two different functions of the poem, one for its maker and another for its reader. Yet his comments on "A Change of Air" in 1964 confirm the observation that he still sees the poem as a parable. At no time does he repudiate the didactic credo expressed in 1944 by Caliban for the "dedicated dramatist":

> Ultimately, what other aim and justification has he, what else exactly *is* the artistic gift which he is forbidden to hide, if not to make you unforgettably conscious of the ungarnished offended gap between what you so questionably are and what you are commanded without any question to become . . . ?[20]

If the parable-maker succeeds in making his reader "unforgettably conscious," he has done his job. In 1956 Auden's terms are religious, but his point is analogous. Even when a poem is conceived as a rite of verbal homage, it can have nothing to do with "God as Redeemer."[21] The road to redemption always runs just outside the province of poetry.

If this is Auden's theory,[22] it is worth while to examine

[20] *CP*, 400.

[21] *Making, Knowing, and Judging,* 30. DH, 57.

[22] Though it is not relevant in the present context, Auden can also present an analysis of the poem considered as an autonomous entity separated from both maker and reader. Cleanth Brooks rightly points out the congruence between such analyses by Auden and the formalist conception of poetry. See "W. H. Auden as Critic," *Kenyon Review,* xxvi (Winter 1964), 173-189.

briefly his usual practice at different times in his career. He himself is conscious that:

> The writing of poetry is always a more complex thing than any theory we may have about it. We write first and use the theory afterwards to justify the particular kind of poetry we like and the particular things about poetry in general which we think we like.[23]

In general, Auden has followed his own admonitions on the importance of consciousness so well that his theory never lags far behind his practice. However, a special situation exists in the poems he wrote before his basic commitment to parable didactics around 1935. In these early poems he exhibited more trust in the efficaciousness of words than he later found acceptable. His basic didactic impulse frequently expressed itself with "The preacher's loose immodest tone" he was to disown in "New Year Letter" (1941).[24] His most frequent exhortation was that the reader should step out of the narrow confines of his ordinary vision for the sake of a detached re-evaluation of himself and his time. "Consider" (1930) is a typical poem of this period, beginning, "Consider this and in our time/ As the hawk sees it or the helmeted airman."[25] In the first of three sections he attempts to capture the reader's interest in a few ominous and suggestive images of the contemporary social climate. The second section, moving closer to home, is addressed to Death, the "supreme Antagonist," who has not only led earlier civilizations to self-destruction, but also at the present time commands nu-

[23] "Pope," in *From Anne to Victoria*, ed. Bonamy Dobrée (New York, 1937), 96. Reprinted in *Essays in Criticism*, 1 (July 1951), 214.
[24] *CP*, 271.
[25] *CP*, 27.

merous admirers. The third stanza is a direct and caustic attack on the reader as one of Death's admirers: "Seekers after happiness, all who follow/ The convolutions of your simple wish,/ It is later than you think." The poem assaults the reader's consciousness in order to sting him, if possible, into some kind of action. Yet no particular course of action is recommended, for in effect the poet says, "Consider, and if this is the way things are, something must be done before it is too late."

This same didactic intent to make the reader conscious of his involvement with existing personal and social problems pervades all the types of poems Auden wrote in the decade of the 1930's. However, his frontal attacks on the reader had mostly disappeared by 1935 when he became conscious that you can only tell people parables. He could still, from time to time, offer transparent advice to the reader, but for the purpose of turning him back on himself, as in "The Witnesses," an extract from *The Dog Beneath the Skin* (1935).

> Look in your heart and see:
>   There lies the answer.
> Though the heart like a clever
>   Conjurer or dancer
> Deceive you often into many
>   A curious sleight
> And motives like stowaways
>   Are found too late.[26]

Usually Auden calls the reader's attention to the symptoms of a prevailing disease; a few times he goes on to outline alternatives between which the reader must make his conscious choice. In "Spain 1937," he insists on the

[26] *CP*, 185.

necessity for a decision which will determine the future of an entire civilization. Life, or History, speaks:

"What's your proposal? To build the Just City? I will.
I agree. Or is it the suicide pact, the romantic
           Death? Very well, I accept, for
I am your choice, your decision: yes, I am Spain."[27]

The closest Auden comes to propagandizing is to suggest that "Love" is the answer to the dilemmas he sees both in individuals and society. A number of poems are, in effect, attempts to define how Love might become the basis for an ethic. But until his return to Christianity about 1940, the concept remains so vague and uncertain, apparently even to Auden himself, that the reader, if he sought one, could find no positive program for action.

The reason for the insistent and sometimes bitter tone of Auden's didacticism in the early part of this decade is best summarized in his evaluation of the Buchmanite Group movement at Oxford. Here in 1934 Auden is turning back on his own origins to criticize the appeal of the Group Movement to unthinking individuals who share his middle-class education and upbringing:

Today the light which has been shed by Freud and Marx on the motivation of thought makes it criminal to be uncritical, and no movement, secular or religious, which is afraid to examine dispassionately and acknowlege openly what self-interest would make it want to believe, is worthy of anything but contempt.[28]

Auden's demand in his poetry is precisely this same starkly critical self-awareness on the part of the reader.

[27] CP, 183.
[28] "The Group Movement and the Middle Classes," in *Oxford and the Groups,* ed. Richard Crossman (Oxford, 1934), 90.

By the decade of the 1940's the vehemence has vanished from Auden's tone. He approaches human lives and events sympathetically: "Centring the eye on their essential human element," as he says in "The Model" (1945).[29] The "Occasional Poems" section in *Another Time* (1940), which includes the famous "In Memory of W. B. Yeats" and "Herman Melville," are skilled exercises in poetry as literary criticism, but more directly they are sympathetic studies of the human problems each man faced in order to produce his art. They affirm the power of the "free man" to praise, despite "the prison of his days."[30] These poems serve Auden's didactic purpose in reaffirming the conviction that human beings can transcend their problems, at least in the sense of being able to transform suffering into art.

Since around 1941, Auden has directed the reader's attention more consistently to the problems of the human individual rather than the collectively human social order. His reconversion to Christianity about this time put him in contact with a conceptual framework which could give "Love" a coherent meaning and relevance to relationships between people. The terms he uses are largely borrowed from Kierkegaard, but he is careful to avoid propagandistic assertion of them. He is more than ever conscious that art, if it can affect the actual, historical world outside itself, must do so indirectly. Joseph Warren Beach imputes a false motive to Auden when, in commenting on "Danse Macabre" (1940), he suggests: "The strategy of the thing is all wrong for a poet wishing to win us over to the Christian point of view."[31] This com-

[29] *CP*, 46.
[30] *CP*, 51.
[31] *Auden Canon*, 202.

[49]

ment is simply irrelevant to Auden's apparent intention, for while it would be ineffective for propaganda, the strategy of the poem *is* appropriate to his didactic poetics. The speaker is one of Auden's "lunatic clergymen," who, like the Vicar in *The Dog Beneath the Skin*, believes he is called to eradicate the Devil and incidentally the human race. The poem is a parable, which will have a different significance for every reader.[32] To arrive at his own understanding the reader must question who precisely is the "Devil" in this poem and in his own life. The process of questioning might ultimately lead a reader, as it has Auden himself, to accept a Christian view of the world, but that eventuality is outside the poem's intention and its achievement.

Similarly, *The Age of Anxiety* (1947) sympathetically studies the problem of four different types of human personality as they attempt to deal with the inescapable anxiety in time that Kierkegaard described, but it foresees no truly religious solution for their problem. Insofar as the Divine dimension enters the poem, it is to emphasize the distance of this world and these people from salvation. The closest they can come to recognizing a Christian belief in God is to envision an oversized father image: "Our lost dad,/ Our colossal father."[33] Like St. Augustine's *Confessions*, Auden's poem demonstrates that human beings are perpetually restless unless they can find a faith in the Timeless, but unlike that work, it suggests no path by which one could reach a spiritual home.

Among the major works of this decade only *For the Time Being: A Christmas Oratorio* depends on explicitly Christian terms, and here Auden is careful to emphasize

32 "K," *The Mid-Century*, No. 17 (Fall 1960), 3. DH, 160.
33 *The Age of Anxiety*, 104.

THE POETICS OF PARABLE

the distance of the world of the Incarnation from our own. St. Joseph must bear the burden of the Absurd by suffering the sympathies of a barroom crowd which sees him as a cuckold; Herod is a perplexed liberal politician who cannot comprehend the phenomenon before him. Particularly in Herod's speech and Caesar's "Fugal-Chorus" Auden demonstrates the futility of locating the ultimate significance of life in material progress; the poem as a whole, however, is not an exhortation but a celebration of the Divine Birth and a definition of its relevance. Auden is fully conscious that "If we try to treat art as magic, we produce, not great works of art, but only dishonest and insufferably earnest and boring Agit-Prop for Christianity, Communism, Free Enterprise or what have you."[34]

The parabolic didacticism of these long poems is supported by a new epistemological concept of "negative knowledge." Because men are separated from God or the Absolute by a barrier of human limitations, no man can dare to define the nature of ultimate reality. We know the Timeless only by the metaphorical means of negating all we know of the time-bound, which is all we know. Hence, the chorus in *For the Time Being* laments: "O where is the garden of Being that is only known in Existence/ As the command to be never there . . . ?"[35] Literally, then, the Eternal as we can know it is "imagined." Similarly, at the culmination of "The Sea and the Mirror," Auden can suggest that art, the product of the human imagination, is a "feebly figurative sign" indirectly reminding us of "Wholly Other Life."[36] And *The Age of Anxiety* can describe us as:

[34] "Squares and Oblongs," 174.
[35] CP, 413.
[36] CP, 402.

[51]

Temporals pleading for eternal life with
The infinite impetus of anxious spirits,
Finite in fact yet refusing to be real,
Wanting our own way, unwilling to say Yes
To the Self-So which is the same at all times,
That Always-Opposite which is the whole subject
Of our not-knowing.[37]

In this richly metaphysical verse, the propagandists—the Romantic, the Fascist, or even the Christian literalist—once again stand implicitly condemned.

In the 1950's Auden essentially continues the didactic practices of the preceding decade. He seldom depends explicitly on the religious terms that he might be expected to propagandize, and he consistently avoids sermonizing. In "Vespers," for example, two citizens meet at dusk in the perspective of "Adam's Grave," the hill overlooking their city. Each reveals what his citizenship in this earthly city means to him. The "I" of the poem is an aesthetic "Arcadian"; his anti-type is a materialist "Utopian." The main body of the poem develops through specific contrasts the complete incompatibility of their values. Yet their meeting, as he meditates about it, seems to the speaker more than a "fortuitous intersection of life-paths, loyal to different fibs." He suggests that it is "also a rendezvous between accomplices who, in spite of themselves, cannot resist meeting":

to remind the other (do both, at bottom, desire truth?) of that half of their secret which he would most like to forget,
forcing us both, for a fraction of a second, to remem-

[37] *The Age of Anxiety*, 137.

ber our victim (but for him I could forget the blood,
but for me he could forget the innocence)

on whose immolation (call him Abel, Remus, whom
you will, it is one Sin Offering) arcadias, utopias, our
dear old bag of a democracy, are alike founded:

For without a cement of blood (it must be human,
it must be innocent) no secular wall will safely stand.[38]

Auden is not exhorting the reader to become Christian;
he is attempting to find poetic terms for defining the
nature and relevance of the Crucifixion. In fact, outside
the implications of its inclusion in the sequence entitled
"Horae Canonicae," the poem allows for interpretation in
other than strictly Christian terms. In the dramatic situation of the poem, the reader is led to identify himself
with the Arcadian "I," who, through pondering the significance of his meeting with his anti-type as a citizen,
is reminded that both of them, and indeed the earthly
city itself, depend for their continued existence on the
kind of sacrifice embodied in Christ's death. The poem
does imply that insofar as both the Arcadian and the
Utopian "desire truth," they will become conscious of
a religious dimension which overarches their limited human philosophies; however, it specifically avoids telling
the reader what his citizenship should be or what he
should will to become. Auden is more confident about
the terms of which he wants the reader to become conscious, but he still practices the same kind of didactic
restraint he outlined earlier.

The new note in Auden's poetry at the end of the
1950's lies not in a change in his basic didactic poetics,
but in the significantly greater restriction he seems to

[38] *The Shield of Achilles* (New York, 1955), 79-80.

place on the poetic use of words for didactic purposes. This increased restraint on the poet's imagination appears in conjunction with a new treatment of nature. Through the "Bucolics" in *The Shield of Achilles,* Auden most often used nature as an external landscape through which to project the hidden inner character of some human type. In *Homage to Clio* (1960), however, a few poems present an untransformed nature basically indifferent to human values. "First Things First," for example, retells the experience of hearing a storm and derives a moral in a surprisingly conventional way:

> Grateful, I slept till a morning that would not say
> How much it believed of what I said the storm
>   had said
> But quietly drew my attention to what had been
>   done
> —So many cubic metres the more in my cistern
> Against a leonine summer—putting first things
>   first:
> Thousands have lived without love, not one without water.[39]

In effect, this poem suggests that Auden is carrying the anti-Romantic position nearer its logical extreme. Now even what the poet feels moved to say about the storm, or nature in general, is untrustworthy; he can only feel sure of the barest physical facts, uninterpreted by the imagination. Perhaps the increasing number of prose-poems in Auden's recent volumes embodies another extension of anti-Romanticism into a new sphere. The epigraph to Part II of *Homage to Clio* may be, in its jocular way, revealing:

[39] *Homage to Clio* (New York, 1960), 57.

> Although you be, as I am, one of those
> Who feel a Christian ought to write in Prose,
> For Poetry is Magic—born in sin, you
> May read it to exorcise the Gentile in you.[40]

Not content to write poetry which avoids magic or propaganda, as much as poetry can avoid them, Auden now seems to feel that perhaps he ought to eschew poetry altogether. Only in time will we know how serious Auden is about this increased restraint.

Such, then, is Auden's characteristic theory and practice of didacticism to date. In his latest affirmation of his position Auden says of the reader's experience of the poem: "Before he is aware of any other qualities it may have, I want his reaction to be: 'That's true' or, better still, 'That's true: now, why didn't I think of it for myself?' To secure this effect I am prepared to sacrifice a great many poetic pleasures and excitements."[41] Once the reader has acknowledged the presence of a truth, the poem has accomplished all it can do in leading him to reflect on it seriously, in Spender's sense of the word.

The notion of restricted didacticism does have one great danger: the poem may have no impact on the reader at all. It may hold up a mirror for the reader to see himself or his world more clearly, but he may keep his eyes closed. Auden has been aware of this problem as is evident from his scornful attack on the "highbrow" reader:

> The low-brow says: "I don't like poetry. It requires too much effort to understand and I'm afraid that if I learnt exactly what I feel, it would make me most uncomfortable." He is in the wrong, of course, but not so

[40] *Homage*, [51].
[41] "Symposium," *Kenyon Review*, XXVI (Winter 1964), 207. Reprinted in *The Contemporary Poet*, ed. Anthony Ostroff, 185-186.

much in the wrong as the high-brow whose gifts make the effort to understand very little and who, having learned what he feels, is not at all uncomfortable, only interested.[42]

To combat this tendency in his readers, Auden has often relied on the devices of satire to jolt his audience into a real reconsideration of themselves and their world. Conventionally, satire is the holding up of human vices to ridicule or attack. To analyze Auden's use of satire as a didactic strategy, we must delineate the criticism he apparently intended and the standard against which he measures the object of attack. We will find that Auden's search for satirical standards is, in effect, a search for didactic content.

As Auden insisted again and again, it is difficult for a modern poet to establish any kind of rapport with his audience. Still more difficult to achieve is sufficient agreement on questions of value to allow the satirist to share standards with any sizable audience. The modern world has a paucity of shared symbols; the only catholicity is one of disagreement. As a result, the problem of finding a vantage point for critical measurement of the status quo is closely related to the problem of locating an audience.

In his early poems, say those before 1935, the audience he felt he could reach was largely limited to his college contemporaries. One would expect that he could find agreement on satiric standards more easily in this relatively homogeneous group. Indeed, the poems of this period are the most vehement in attacking things as they are. Auden insists that *something* must be done soon and

[42] "Squares and Oblongs," 180.

draws on three major reservoirs of imagery to bring the point home to his audience. Post-Freudian psychology, primarily derived from Homer Lane and Georg Groddeck, provides him with the terms to particularize and protest the prevailing psychic sickness: "The intolerable neural itch,/ The exhaustion of weaning, the liar's quinsy,/ And the distortions of ingrown virginity."[43] To protest the failure of the social order Auden relies primarily on the landscape of abandoned and rusting machinery which was nearly his trademark in the early poems.

> Get there if you can and see the land you once
>   were proud to own
> Though the roads have almost vanished and
>   the expresses never run:
>
> Smokeless chimneys, damaged bridges, rotting
>   wharves and choked canals,
> Tramlines buckled, smashed trucks lying on their
>   side across the rails;
>
> .   .   .   .
>
> If we really want to live, we'd better start at once
>   to try;
> If we don't, it doesn't matter, but we'd better
>   start to die.[44]

The third fund of imagery, that of war and the frontier, serves to emphasize the importance of what is at stake

[43] "Petition," CP, 110.
[44] Poems (London, 1930), 66, 70. Not reprinted in CP. The closing couplet is an interesting example of the early Auden's control over rhetoric. The neat parallelism of the two lines violates their sense: If we are not willing to try to live, that itself is a sign that we are already dying. The "senselessness" of acquiescing to such a death is a neat reinforcement of Auden's satire.

and the urgency of the situation. It is never very clear in these poems just who is fighting and for what. At most it is a sort of hereditary feud as in "Paid on Both Sides" (1930). Still, the threatening possibility of defeat by an uncertainly known enemy is a successful matrix of imagery to communicate the sense of urgency Auden intends.

Though these patterns of imagery are useful for Auden to define in general terms what is wrong with the contemporary world, they do not reveal the basic standard by which he determines that something is wrong. Basically, the present world is found wanting because it violates an ideal world—in these early poems, the ideal world of childhood. Thus the early Auden commonly relies on nostalgia for a simpler, nobler age and rejection of the adult world from the perspective of an adolescent. In the volume, *Poems* (1930), for example, a yearning for an ideal world seems to exist in suspension with an anti-Romantic denial that it is attainable.[45] Out of the tension between the two comes Auden's particular type of satire. He himself gives an excellent description in defining Byronic satire, which seems to him like that of two other poets he has admired, John Skelton and D. H. Lawrence:

It is the weapon of the rebel who refuses to accept conventional laws and pieties as binding or worthy of respect. Instead of speaking in the name of all well-educated and sensible people, it speaks in the name of the individual whose innocence of vision has not been corrupted by education and social convention. Where Pope, so to speak, says, "The Emperor is wearing a

[45] See, for example, poems II and XVI.

[58]

celluloid collar," Byron says, "The Emperor has no clothes."[46]

Pope is, of course, a satirist of a high order, but ostensibly he would be satisfied if men acted more civilized. Auden's early satire is of the Byronic sort; insofar as it calls for anything, it demands a whole new world.

Though satire is necessarily didactic, the converse is not true and Auden has gone on to exploit many more didactic strategies. *The Rake's Progress* (1951) can serve his underlying didactic purpose by spinning a moral fable in which only a few scenes are clearly satiric. "First Things First," discussed earlier, presents its didactic point by intentionally naïve observation of nature, leading to an obvious moral. Instead of using the perspective of the ideal world to reject the real, most of Auden's poems since the middle 1930's attempt to define the proper relationship between them. The two are distinct, but essentially related. The ideal world is the dimension which reveals what the real world is not, but should be. Auden consistently rejects the Romantic notion that the ideal is attainable, even imaginatively; instead the ideal is that which we, as humans, should strive after with full knowledge that it is not attainable on earth. In accordance with his poetics, Auden refrains from consistently advocating any particular ideal. Rather, he is concerned with showing the reader how the two worlds are necessarily related in a kind of "reciprocity."[47] Accordingly the representations of the ideal in these mature poems are

[46] "The Life of That-There Poet," *New Yorker*, xxxiv (April 26, 1958), 136. More recently Auden finds Byron, at least in *Don Juan*, comic rather than satiric; see DH, 388-390. An adapted form of this quotation is applied to D. H. Lawrence, DH, 295.

[47] "Conversation on Cornelia Street: Dialogue with W. H. Auden," *Accent*, x (August 1949), 51.

manifold. It may be a mountain,[48] the Good Place,[49] the Hidden Law,[50] Atlantis,[51] Ariel,[52] the Crucified Christ.[53] Especially in the poems of the 1950's the dimension of the ideal may not appear explicitly, but its presence is often indicated by the terms in which the poem treats the actual world. Auden projects great sympathy toward the human creatures he describes. In the perspective of the ideal or absolute, no human being is outstandingly good.

Auden has searched out still more non-satiric devices to trap the reader into really seeing something in the mirror of the poem. Poems like "Petition" (1930) and "Perhaps" (1933)[54] are startling because the ostensibly atheistic Auden has cast them in the form and syntax of prayer. Admittedly the beings addressed seem rather shadowy: "Sir, no man's enemy" and "O Love, the interest itself in thoughtless Heaven" respectively. But this very lack of focus helps to indicate the didactic function of the "prayers." By the first person plural pronoun the reader is drawn into the position of admitting that we, and hence he, do stand in need of prayer, of revitalizing, even if we are not too sure where "New styles of architecture" and "a change of heart" can come from. The poet has manipulated point of view so that the reader must assent to self-condemnation or refuse to read the poem.

Another technique for luring the reader into encounter

[48] "Now the leaves are falling fast" (1936), *CP*, 217-218.
[49] "The Prophets" (1940), *CP*, 99-100.
[50] "Aera sub Lege" (1941), *CP*, 117-118.
[51] "Atlantis" (1945), *CP*, 20-22.
[52] "The Sea and the Mirror" (1944), *CP*, 351-404.
[53] "Horae Canonicae" (1951-1955), *The Shield of Achilles*, 63-84, or "Friday's Child" (1960), *Homage to Clio*, 77-78.
[54] *CP*, 110 and 89, respectively.

with the poem has earned Auden considerable harsh criticism. It is the arrangement of short poems in his volumes of *Collected Poetry* (1945) and *Collected Shorter Poems* (1950) in alphabetical order by first lines, with no indication of the original order of composition or publication. Joseph Warren Beach's basic objection to this procedure runs as follows: "For the reader who wishes earnestly to get at the original intent of a given poem, it is often a matter of real importance to determine the date of composition in order that it may be understood in terms of the theories, prepossessions, and attitudes prevailing with the author at the time of writing."[55] Beach goes on to say that although he does not mean to imply that "this curious system of contextual obfuscation was deliberately designed by the poet to confuse and deceive his reader,"[56] we must recognize, he thinks, that mystification was a favorite game of Auden's from the start. Beach seems to me to have quite missed the point here. One response that Auden wishes to save his poems from is precisely this concern for original intention. The concern for isolating and describing original intent is certainly a valid quest for a scholar to pursue, but clearly Auden has aimed all along at an audience of more than scholars. He wants the poem to affect the reader. He wants to discourage the general reader from categorizing the mirror instead of seeing something in it.

These collected volumes were not the first in which Auden employed this arrangement of poems to circumvent the defenses that he could predict in his readers. In an earlier volume, which was, significantly enough, designed as a teaching anthology, he used the same edi-

[55] *Auden Canon*, 12.
[56] *Auden Canon*, 15.

[61]

torial technique. The justification the editors there make for the alphabetical arrangement can apply as well to Auden's later use of the same device. To poetry, the authors say, "the first approach should be with an open mind, free from the bias of great names and literary influences, the first impression that of a human activity, independent of period and unconfined in subject."[57] Auden consciously employed this editorial device in an attempt to increase the effectiveness of the poetry in reaching the audience. In effect, he is trying to save his audience from their own comfortable illusions. It is interesting to note that a recent volume of poems selected by Auden, issued by Penguin in 1958 and Random House in 1959, presents poems in clearly defined chronological order. A note in the Penguin volume indicates not that Auden has changed his understanding of how poems are to be read, but that he has yielded to unfavorable criticism.

An analogous trick for circumventing the reader's defenses is the suppression of titles. Not until *Another Time* (1940) did Auden begin using titles in his volumes. From the beginning he was quite aware that a reader can use a title as well as a date of origin to call forth a bias in his mind and avoid serious looking in the mirror of the poem. In his collected volumes Auden did title poems that had originally appeared with none, but he took care either to employ a phrase from the poem itself or to introduce a phrase so far out of its context that the reader had to supply a large stretch of the imagination to include the title in his experience of the poem. Monroe Spears accurately describes the latter sort of title as

[57] *The Poet's Tongue*, ed. W. H. Auden and John Garrett, one-volume ed. (London, 1935), x.

"highly colloquial and often flip."[58] Even if we assent to Spears's rejection of "deplorably facetious" titles, we must recognize that they are facetious with the deliberate artistry of a teacher.

These strategies in presenting the poem are additional manifestations of Auden's basically didactic poetics. His theoretical pronouncements over the years and his actual poetic practice agree in indicating his primary concern with the poem as parable. His anti-Romanticism should also be evident. He is committed to the poem not primarily as a means to self-expression, with the audience, as it were, overhearing, but to the poem as a performance for the sake of impact on that audience. He hopes that his words will stimulate some tangible moral change, but he refuses to tell his reader what to think or do. Any reorientation in the reader's life as a result of his encounter with the poem must be left to him. What Auden can and does do as a poet, and even as an anthologizer, is to marshal all the devices he knows to ensure that there will be an encounter. What we need to consider next is how Auden can implement his didactic aims—how he can shape a poetic message for a wide variety of readers but stimulate each to reflect in his own personal terms.

[58] *Poetry of Auden*, 199, 203.

CHAPTER III

ALLEGORY

AUDEN remarks that to write poetry, two quite distinct gifts are required: "a love of language and a private vision of the public world."[1] He himself seems always to have had the love of language and a fascination with its use in difficult circumstances, like verse forms as complex as the canzone and sestina. Formulating a private vision of the public world, on the other hand, has been one of his greatest problems. In the way he has solved it, I think, lies the root of his insistence on anti-Romantic themes and techniques in his poetry.

The problem of making contact between the private and the public worlds is aggravated by the kind of public world created by modern technological civilization.

> For poetry to take an interest in and be capable of dealing with a subject, the latter must possess three qualities: personality, power, and virtue or wickedness. . . .
>
> But the machine divorced power from person: nature becomes an impersonal slave. . . . Even the personal influence a public figure can exert depends less on his personality than on the printing-presses and loudspeakers he can command. . . . A natural ease of communication between artist and audience requires that the unity of power and person which is the aesthetic subject be publicly manifest, but in such a civilization they are united only on the private level.[2]

[1] "Foreword," to Robert Horan, A Beginning (New Haven, 1948), 7.
[2] "The Word and the Machine," Encounter, II (April 1954), 3-4. See DH, 80-81, for a restatement of the same point.

As a result, however much he may desire it, the poet has no "public" subjects; he can have no personal relation to public figures or events. Similarly, there is no coherent public for poetry; the only catholicity is one of isolation once the connection between public and private has broken down. The poet must speak to his audience as a random collection of those particular individuals who happen to read his poems. If he makes reference to the public world at all, it must be to that world as it is felt by the individual man, who is isolated from it:

> If I meet an illiterate peasant we may not be able to say much to each other, but if we both meet a public official, we share the same feeling of suspicion; neither of us will trust him further than we can throw a grand piano. If we enter a government building, we share the same feeling of apprehension that perhaps we shall never get out. Whatever the cultural differences between us, we both sniff in an official world the smell of the unreality in which persons are treated as statistics.[3]

Thus, fragmented though the public world is, it does offer some area of common attitude—the negative one of distrust. There remain also a few fairly common frames of reference, like nursery rimes and fairy tales, that Auden has exploited as much as possible. But even these limited sources of common background and attitude provide no basis for communication unless the poet can bring his personal vision into contact with them.

For Auden, the nature of his private world, at least initially, offered even more of a problem than the fragmented public world. In scattered autobiographical articles

[3] "The Dyer's Hand," 300-301. *DH*, 88, recast in the third person for greater objectivity.

he consistently describes himself in his youth as isolated in an introvert's dream world that would be difficult to communicate to anyone, let alone an appreciable audience. Up to the age of fifteen, he says, "I had been the sole autocratic inhabitant of a dream country of lead mines, narrow-gauge tramways, and overshot waterwheels. But in March, 1922, I decided to become a poet."[4] Starting from this fantasy world, the attitudes toward life and art that Auden brought to this new-found ambition are strikingly Romantic:

> I have yet to meet a poetry-lover under thirty who was not an introvert, or an introvert who was not unhappy in adolescence. At school, particularly, maybe, if, as in my case, it is a boarding school, he sees the extrovert successful, happy, and good and himself unpopular or neglected. . . . He turns away from the human to the non-human. . . . The growing life within him will express itself in a devotion to music and thoughts upon mutability and death. Art for him will be something infinitely precious, pessimistic, and hostile to life. If it speaks of love, it must be love frustrated, for all success seems to him noisy and vulgar.[5]

Auden seems to be describing here the Romantic self-dramatization of an introvert trying to make the best use of his isolation. But unlike the English Romantics, he turned for consolation, in his earliest poetry, to the non-human world of machinery. Auden evidently felt himself driven by strong emotional attachments and disappointments, but in a poetic world populated by machinery he

[4] "A Literary Transference," *Southern Review*, VI (Summer 1940), 78.
[5] *Ibid.*, 78-79.

could envision the placidity and self-sufficient power he aspired to and missed in himself. "The Traction Engine," written by 1926, concludes with this wistfully affectionate description of a rusty engine:

> Unfeeling, uncaring; imaginings
> Mar not the future; no past sick memory clings,
> Yet it seems well to deserve the love we reserve
> For animate things.[6]

More typically Romantic is the attitude Auden expresses toward vulgar success in the human world of society; it is reminiscent of Baudelaire's rejection of bourgeois success. Echoes of Baudelaire's brand of Romanticism persisted in Auden's work at least through *The Orators* in 1932. "Journal of an Airman" particularly bears a notable resemblance to Baudelaire's *Intimate Journals*, which Christopher Isherwood translated in 1930, and also to Rimbaud's *Les Illuminations*.[7] In addition, we recall that the young Rimbaud, whose present "guilt demands," and Baudelaire are among the nine judges Auden selects for himself in "New Year Letter."[8]

Traces of his adolescent Romanticism remained in some of Auden's poetry for years afterward, but an important change came over his basic attitudes when T. S. Eliot won the "Battle of Oxford" in 1926.[9] Auden reveals something of the substance of this transformation in another description of his adolescent self:

[6] Quoted from Christopher Isherwood, *Lions and Shadows* (Norfolk, Connecticut, 1947), 186 (first published in 1937).

[7] See Auden's quotation from the latter in *The Enchafèd Flood* (London, 1951), 33.

[8] CP, 270.

[9] "A Literary Transference," 80.

The son of book-loving, Anglo-Catholic parents of the professional class, the youngest of three brothers, I was—and in most respects still am—mentally precocious, physically backward, short-sighted, a rabbit at all games, very untidy and grubby, a nail-biter, a physical coward, dishonest, sentimental, with no community sense whatever, in fact a typical little highbrow and difficult child.[10]

The tone of this self-analysis itself embodies the change. This is debunking—exaggeratedly "honest" self-criticism. In his own witty manner Auden is out to deflate any flattering image of his earlier self. He applies to himself, as indeed to most of the subjects that come before his scrutiny, the same "detached irreverence" he has noted in Byron.[11] Nonetheless, Auden's consistently acute self-understanding suggests that even such studied self-disparagement has some justification.

Perhaps the most striking evidence of his ability to relate his new self-knowledge to the public world lies in the speed with which he recognized Romanticism as the demon to be fought both within and outside himself. By the time of *Oxford Poetry*, 1927, which he edited and introduced with C. Day Lewis, Auden had identified Romantic subjectivity as the basic divisive force threatening the modern world and psyche. Here, in the year after he had accepted the decisive influence of Eliot, Auden attacks "our *sauve-qui-peut*, that acedia and unabashed glorification of the subjective so prominent in the world since the Reformation."[12] This distrust of the self-centered, the subjective, and the Romantic has remained

---

[10] "Honour [Gresham's School, Holt]," in *The Old School*, ed. Graham Greene (London, 1934), 9.
[11] "The Life of That-There Poet," 137.
[12] (Oxford, 1927), v.

endemic in Auden's views ever since in his anti-fascist politics, his religious orthodoxy, and his didactic poetics. In his practice of poetry, as well, his insistent reliance on defined and established poetic forms rather than "free verse" is an analogous curbing of the purely subjective imagination. Similarly he relies on the intellectual control implicit in allegory to search out the universal human aspects of his unique personal experience.

Though the substance of the transformation begun around 1926 is reasonably clear, the mechanism is hard to recover. Auden himself, commenting on Baudelaire, gives what is probably the best description possible outside the context of a full critical biography or an autobiography:

> Sooner or later, the change comes to all and, once this happens, it is decisive and irrevocable—for, whatever the field, once the mind becomes conscious of alternatives, retreat into habit is cut off; either a man must make a deliberate choice (that is to say, become a critic as well as an actor) or become paralysed. Reliance on others is only possible in so far as their authority can be recognized, i.e. chosen.[13]

In Auden's case, it is clear that his conscious choice was to reject his adolescent Romantic self. As a check on its unrestrained subjectivity he turned to several parallel kinds of control. As philosophical and thematic groundwork for his poetry he has successively adopted the more or less well-defined formulations of human existence that comprise Freudian psychology, Marxist theory of history, and Christian orthodoxy. In his expository

[13] "Introduction" to *The Intimate Journals of Charles Baudelaire*, trans. Christopher Isherwood (Boston, 1957), xx. First published in 1947.

prose he has relied on conscious reasoning, clarifying distinctions by defining extremes. In his poetry an analogous characteristic is allegory. The function of all these anti-Romantic stances is to restrain uncontrolled subjectivity. Through examining his experience in the light of reason or even dogma, the poet can become aware of what is unique to himself and what he shares with other human beings. By concentrating his artistic energy on what is shared, he brings the particular into relation with the general and the private into contact with the public.

The type of allegory Auden characteristically employs in his poetry is most easily approached through his expository prose. Auden's is a particularly schematic imagination that reveals itself more starkly in his prose than in his verse. His habitual attack on a subject is to distinguish two equal but opposite extremes that are relevant, and, employing his pungent wit, to describe them in their most extreme forms. In religious terms he may isolate two basic heresies, monism and dualism; in relation to the audience for poetry, the opposites may be the highbrow and the lowbrow; in political theory, he may delineate the competing claims of freedom of action versus equality of treatment. As Auden candidly admits in developing these oppositions, neither extreme need ever have existed, but he "can construct a Platonic idea of both."[14] The technique of abstracting these idealized opposites has the advantage of being adaptable to any subject. Though it always oversimplifies, it can push whatever tendencies the author sees in his subject out to their logical extremes where they can be easily grasped by the intellect. It is, in fact, an effective pedagogical device.

[14] "Criticism in a Mass Society," in *The Intent of the Critic*, ed. Donald A. Stauffer (Princeton, 1941), 129.

Once he has abstracted the opposites, Auden's point is nearly always that neither extreme is satisfactory. Some balance or reconciliation of the opposites is desirable. The process of reaching this conclusion is virtually tautological, for he isolated the opposites originally as positions so extreme that they could hardly be acceptable to any reasonable man. However, the value of the process of isolating and then rejecting both extremes is that Auden can make his comment on the subject while leaving to the reader the precise formulation of the reconciliation of the extremes. The device thus serves in Auden's expository prose an anti-Romantic purpose analogous to the strategy of his didactic poetics. He need not endorse any specific action so long as he can show that each extreme is destructive when carried to the exclusion of its opposite. A recent comment on Christian groups can illustrate the way in which he can raise issues without defending any particular position except the objective and reasonable:

> One might say that, in conjugating the present tense of the verb *to be*, catholicism concentrates on the plural, protestantism on the singular. But authentic human existence demands that equal meaning and value be given to both singular and plural, all three persons, all three genders. Thus, protestantism is correct in affirming that the *We are* of society expresses a false identity unless each of its members can say *I am*; catholicism is correct in affirming that the individual who will not or cannot join with others in saying *We* does not know the meaning of *I*.[15]

[15] "Greatness Finding Itself," *The Mid-Century*, No. XIII (June 1960), 17-18.

Occasionally Auden carries this schematization beyond dualities to three- and even four-sided patterns. He often employs tables and parallel epigrammatic lists to reinforce visually the contrasts between the factors he is isolating. In 1939, for example, he compares the Medieval, Puritan, and Romantic views on three aspects of the nature of society.[16] The neatness of the scheme is emphasized by parallel lists phrased in as nearly balanced terms as possible. Even in these more complex formulaic analyses, however, Auden's interest is the same, i.e., to suggest that some composite or reconciliation of extreme positions is needed. Only wholeness and integration can lead to satisfactory human living.[17]

The same schematizing function of the imagination began appearing in Auden's poetry as early as 1930:

So is the fate of the insolent mind that takes
Truth as itself, in homicidal phantasies
Of itself the divine punisher of the world,
In aphasia and general paralysis of the insane.
Or by opposite error also is man deceived,
Seeking a heaven on earth he chases his shadow,
Loses his capital and his nerve in pursuing
What yachtsmen, explorers, climbers and buggers
    are after.[18]

[16] See Auden and J. C. Worsley, *Education Today—and Tomorrow* [Day-to-Day Pamphlets], (London, 1939), 32-34. See also Monroe Spears's description of an interesting chart Auden used at Swarthmore: *Poetry of Auden*, 248-249, n. 45.

[17] As early as 1930 Auden endorses a Jungian concern for psychic integration by condemning false divisions of the human being into higher and lower selves. See Auden's review of *Instinct and Intuition* by G. B. Dibblee, *Criterion*, IX (April 1930), 569.

[18] See "Which of you waking early and watching daybreak," *Poems* (London, 1930), 40-41. Not reprinted in *CP*.

While our primary interest here is in the structural pattern in which Auden casts his thought, we may note that this particular stanza pillories two equally pernicious extremes of Romantic self-glorification: the self-aggrandizing search for an earthly paradise and the self-flattering withdrawal from the world into insanity.[19] When he studies relationships between human beings, Auden expresses himself, almost instinctively, in an analogous scheme of opposites. In "Do Be Careful" (1930), for example, he thus counsels moderation in the developing of a friendship:

> On neither side let foot slip over
> Invading Always, exploring Never,
> For this is hate and this is fear.
>
> On narrowness stand, for sunlight is
> Brightest only on surfaces;
> No anger, no traitor, but peace.[20]

Here, reinforced by the use of capitalized adverbs as substantives, the submerged metaphor pictures a person standing on a mountain ridge or knife edge. On either side of this narrowness lie the opposites which could destroy the human relationship; they are, in fact, the Romantic extremes of all or nothing-at-all advanced as forms of human companionship.

[19] Auden has continued through the years to attack these same human aberrations. The first appears most notably in his portraits of lunatic clergymen like the speaker of "Danse Macabre" (1940), and the second in numerous seekers after the "secular abundant bliss," like Tom Rakewell in *The Rake's Progress* (1951).

[20] *CP*, 151. See also "Two's Company," *CP*, 5. "We All Make Mistakes" (1930) makes the "razor-edge" explicit: *CP*, 152. Alonzo's address to Ferdinand in "The Sea and the Mirror" (1944) uses an analogous image of the tightrope: *CP*, 367.

Auden's later reliance on the scheme of opposites usually involves a slightly different emphasis, though he seems as firmly committed to its use in developing poems. Where the poems of 1930 isolate extremes that are to be avoided, most of his later poems define opposites which need to be held in balance. In "The Sea and the Mirror," for example, both Caliban and Ariel are essential to the mature artist and to his audience. The Arcadian and his anti-type, the Utopian, in "Vespers" (1955) each understands half of the significance of the Crucifixion. Even when Auden is more interested in only one of the opposites, as in "Homage to Clio" (1960), he is careful to recognize the existence of Clio's opposite, man's natural (as opposed to historical) existence, symbolized by Aphrodite and Artemis.

Auden's schematic habit of imagination leads very easily to the practice of allegory. The schematic approach abstracts from any subject exaggerated and simplified entities that are easily grasped by the intellect. When the subject is the nature of a human being, the schematic imagination leads directly to the separation and allegorization of human faculties or emotions. If the subject is human society, differing human philosophies or attitudes are more likely to constitute the poles of the scheme. In his mature poetry as well as his prose the schematic approach assists Auden to develop his most basic theme, the need for reasonable balance between or reconciliation of conflicting extremes.

Auden's constant concern with the unseen, supraphysical significations of events and figures is not what makes him an allegorist, however. The crucial characteristic is his reliance on an organized conceptual understanding of the unseen, as becomes clear when we compare Auden's poetry to a work that employs symbolism as opposed to allegory. In *Moby Dick*, for instance, we see Melville attempting to probe the unknown and mysterious without being able to pin down its nature with any precision. Auden, on the other hand, seems always committed to conceptual formulations of the unknown. Often he borrows the categories and concepts of an existing intellectual framework, whether it be Freudian (as in *The Orators*), Kierkegaardian (as in "New Year Letter"), or Jungian (as in the four-sided analysis of man in *The Age of Anxiety*).[20a] Where there is ambiguity in Auden's poetry, it is not the symbolist's ambiguity, which reflects the artist's inability or unwillingness to define the nature of the unknown. Rather, it is the relatively flat ambiguity of a riddle. The reader grasps the sense of the poem by an act of intellect in identifying the abstract meaning that is signified by the images.[21]

The distinction between allegory and symbolism as it applies to Auden may be further clarified by reference to one of his own comments:

> Allegory is a form of rhetoric, a device for making the abstract concrete; in nearly all successful allegory the images used do in fact have a symbolic value over and above their allegorical use, but that is secondary to the poet's purpose.[22]

[20a] See important article by Edward Callan, "Allegory in *The Age of Anxiety*," *Twentieth Century Literature*, x (January 1965).

[21] Auden seems accurate when he defines himself in Jungian terms as a "thinking-intuitive" type. His ideal reader should, perhaps, be able to respond in the same way. See "A Literary Transference," 80.

[22] "Introduction" to *Poets of the English Language*, ed. Auden and Norman Holmes Pearson, Viking Portable Library, vol. IV (New York, 1950), xix. The introductions in this series were written by Auden and approved by Pearson. Auden's earlier attempt to distinguish between allegory and symbolism is less than successful.

By relying on the "poet's purpose" as the test for the presence of allegory, Auden allows for a certain latitude in the reader's response. Some of his own readers may find images or figures coming to have a numinous quality for them. Such a response might seem particularly appropriate to two figures which appear more than once— the "truly strong man" of the early 1930's[23] and the personified Love prominent in poems later in that decade. In addition to their symbol-like ambiguity, however, these figures serve a clear allegorical purpose as personified reconciliations of conflicting opposites.

Auden asks a great deal of allegory. For the reader to grasp the abstract or public meaning of a poem is not enough. As suggested earlier, his didactic goal requires that the reader become involved in a process of self-assessment which, to be meaningful, must be carried on in specific terms. Hence the allegory must first lead the reader to assent to the truth of a widely applicable insight into human existence. Then, hopefully, he will go on to apply the general truth to himself. As Auden reaffirms in 1962, "The present-day reader of poetry has to make an effort that was not demanded of readers in earlier times; he has to translate what is actually said in a poem into the terms of his analogous experiences."[24] Auden asks that his reader move from the particulars of the poem through its abstract and general significance to

---

He proposes that whether any image is allegorical or symbolic is wholly relative to each reader's response; then he goes on to base his argument on images which are "really symbolic." See "Mimesis and Allegory," *English Institute Annual, 1940*, ed. Rudolf Kirk (New York, 1941), 4-5.

[23] See discussion of this type-figure re *The Ascent of F6* in the succeeding chapter.

[24] "Today's Poet," *Mademoiselle*, LIV (April 1962), 187.

his own personal self-examination. Such complex indirection is necessitated by the poet's desire to avoid self-assertion. To *tell* the reader what to think directly and specifically would be to preach at him. It would also limit the poet's audience to those who thought as he did. On the other hand, to write a poem entirely on the level of generalities without any concrete particulars would run the risk of failing to engage the active attention of any reader, except, perhaps, the habitual seeker after generalities. Auden's anti-Romantic thinking here closely parallels the views expressed by Dr. Johnson and most neo-Classical theorists of poetry.

To construct an allegory that will successfully initiate the process just described, Auden must first locate the right sort of concrete images. Allegory presumes an ideational connection between the particular images of the poem and its theme. There need be no physical or sensuous resemblance between the allegorical image and what it signifies. As a result, no particular image is indispensable to an allegory; that image is best which succeeds in leading the reader to grasp the abstract "truth" the poet has in mind. Traditional and conventional allegorical images like the cross or the hammer and sickle are largely lost to the modern poet because they call forth overly stereotyped responses. Instead he needs in each new poem to find images fresh and arresting enough to reclothe his abstract visions.[25] Ideally these will be sharp and vivid

[25] In his Romantic reading of Auden, John Bayley would test the worth of an Auden poem by "whether or not it is filled with vivid personal apprehensions of things." (*The Romantic Survival* [London, 1957], 156.) With the possible exception of the word "personal" this seems admirable as a quick criterion. Unlike Mr. Bayley, however, I find the vivid particulars important because, without them, the allegorical vision of a poem fails to live. This critic's remarks are often just and stimulating, but, to me, most

particulars that one would not, before the poem, have thought of thinking about. Take the following lines from "Petition" (1932), for example:

> Send to us power and light, a sovereign touch
> Curing the intolerable neural itch,
> The exhaustion of weaning, the liar's quinsy,
> And the distortions of ingrown virginity.[26]

Most readers would pause first at the strangeness and arbitrariness of this list of symptoms. How can such incongruous images be related to each other? In asking this question the reader is on the way to seeing that these physical malfunctions are merely signs of a pervading malaise of soul or psyche. If he is to relate the point of the poem to himself, he must grasp the abstract significance first, unless, perchance, he has the liar's quinsy and is willing to admit the fact to himself. Once he sees that the widespread malaise is Auden's essential interest, he may be able to recognize its particular symptoms in himself. In any case he will see that the individual images are only important insofar as they provide arresting particularizations of the general point.

Perhaps a close analysis of a poem containing this type of allegory may help to define it more closely. "Have a

---

revealing of Auden's work before 1935. See reprinted excerpt in *Auden*, ed. Monroe K. Spears, 79.

[26] *CP*, 110. Recently "A Change of Air" employs a remarkably similar list used in the same way: "Corns, heartburn, sinus headaches, such minor ailments/ Tell of estrangement between your name and you,/ Suggest a change of air." The poem does not ask that any reader have experienced any of these ailments, or all of them, but that he see analogous manifestations of "estrangement" in his own life. See also "Symposium," *Kenyon Review*, xxvi (Winter 1964), for Auden's amusing comments about corns as a psychosomatic ailment.

Good Time" (1932), for example, presents the reader with a "map of the country," whose primary landmarks are a wood, a bay, vats, and a clock.[27] Their importance and the shifting relationships between them are accentuated by their use as rime words in a sestina. It is evident from the envoy to the poem, which shifts the landmarks closer together, that by the end of the poem a new and more integrated vision of "the country" has replaced the original map. The problem that faces the reader is to grasp for himself the allegorized, humanized significance of the landscape and the map. When he encounters the poem by itself, as in the *Collected Poetry*, the reader can be certain only of the general theme—the need for integration of the landscape. He is invited to supply his own inner divisions to identify specifically the landmarks that move closer together when one begins to live more creatively, "following his love."

A less personal way of locating the meaning of this poem is to look at the context of the original publication in *The Orators*. The Airman has just characterized a stuffy and overly literal intellectual: "Of the enemy as philosopher. Talking of intellect-will-sensation as real and separate entities. The Oxford Don: 'I don't feel quite happy about pleasure.'"[28] The link between this comment and the poem is, like the other connections in the volume, implicit and associational, but it sets a context in which we may decipher the allegorical shorthand of the poem. The people who bring the map to the young man are, in a general sense, his elders; they have "lived

[27] *CP*, 155-156.
[28] *The Orators* (London, 1932), 46. For a somewhat different interpretation to which I am indebted, see F. A. Philbrick, "Auden's 'Have a Good Time,'" *Explicator*, IV (December 1945), item 21.

for years, you know, in the country." More specifically, they are his Oxford Dons. The map they bring distinguishes and treats as separate the wood, the place of *sensation* where there resides "a flying trickster" or Cupid; the bay, a sheltered, shallow harbor where one may keep one's *intellect* fit by bathing; and the clock, which indicates to one's *will* when it should exert itself. This basic map implies that one may operate successfully in the country of life by compartmentalizing these separate human faculties. The Dons make it clear that they, who live by the clock, have arranged a proper job for the young man at the vats. These are, presumably, dyer's vats, which serve as an allegorical representation of art. The Dons' manager at the vats is, in literary terms, a respectable publisher or editor. The young man is exhorted to stay away from the pleasurable but dangerous woods and to keep his mind active by bathing in the bay. But restraint is the key to success in the Establishment: "You're sure of a settled job at the vats/ If you keep their hours and live by the clock." Then the young man is ready to face the country: "He arrived at last; it was time by the clock," i.e., he graduated. Once out in the world, however, the young man begins to deviate from the regimen recommended by the Dons: "At the week-ends the divers in the bay/ Distracted his eyes from the bandstand clock" (the clock which set the tempo for him to dance). These divers are deep thinkers, not merely bathers. Also "he came to love/ The moss that grew on the derelict vats." Apparently he began to revere some abandoned or unpopular old artists. By the last stanza the young man has begun to integrate his faculties: "And he has met sketching at the vats/ Guests from the new hotel in the bay." Through the agency of new artists who are associated with the bay, it now seems possible for intellect to be related to art.

> Now curious following his love,
> His pulses differing from the clock,
> Finds consummation in the wood
> And sees for the first time the country.
>
> Sees water in the wood and trees by the bay,
> Hears a clock striking near the vats;
> "This is your country and the home of love."[29]

Intellect, will, and sensation are now brought close together and focused around art; the young man has discovered his own integrated view of the country. This poem encapsulates Auden's allegory. As in traditional allegory, the images are clearly more than simply features of a physical landscape. Their core theme of personal integration is easily available to the interpreter. The specific application of the theme, however, is left to the reader's self-reflection. He may choose to accept the authority of some context external to the poem, as I have done here for the sake of illustration; otherwise, lacking a community of belief, the reader has no frame of reference for specific interpretation except his isolated private self.

However much he hopes the reader will take this final step, the poet can never force its occurrence. What he can do in constructing the poem is to ensure that the reader cannot take poetic particulars as an end in themselves. Hence Auden is prominently concerned with the general and abstract. His poetry has the same characteristic he noted in three writers whom he has admired greatly at different times in his career—William Blake, D. H. Lawrence, and Charles Williams; it is more in-

[29] CP, 156.

terested in states of being than in individuals.[30] We may also recall Auden's criticism of Kenneth Burke's literary theory that in focusing so much attention on ambiguity, it ignored "the general meaning which can be 'not-This-House-but-all-possible-houses.' "[31]

To insist that the reader encounter the general view projected in a poem, Auden marshals masterful control over rhetoric and point of view. We have already noted in "Consider" (1930) his use of the distant perspective of the hawk or helmeted airman to project a panoramic view of a whole civilization. The reader is asked to rise above his local habitation to encompass a broad sweep of "territory." Similarly, "A Summer Night 1933" (1936) incorporates a moon's-eye perspective over the continent of Europe that transcends all parochial distinctions: "Churches and power-station lie/ Alike among earth's fixtures."[32] The point of view may be distant not only in space, but in emotion. "The Watershed" (1928) and "Look, stranger, on this island now" (1936), for example, substitute the detachment of the foreigner for the distance of the hawk. For a similar effect "The Shield of Achilles" (1955) employs contrasts in time by juxtaposing the heroic world of Hephaestos and Thetis with the barbaric world of the concentration camp. "Memorial for the City" (1951) records a dispassionate overview of human civilizations through the eyes of "The crow on the crema-

[30] "Some Notes on D. H. Lawrence," *The Nation*, CLXIV (April 26, 1947), 482. Auden employs the same phrase in "Charles Williams," *Christian Century*, LXXIII (May 2, 1956), 552. In both instances Auden is likening these authors to Blake.

[31] "A Grammar of Assent," 59.

[32] *CP*, 97. Auden readily acknowledges that he learned the distant perspective from his earliest poetic master, Thomas Hardy. See "A Literary Transference," 83.

torium chimney/ And the camera roving the battle."[33]
A number of more recent poems like "The More Loving
One" (1960) locate the persona on the ground looking
up at the vastness of the stars.

This use of point of view to move the reader to a broad
perspective on his world is capable of almost infinite
variety. "The Unknown Citizen" (1940), though rather
heavy-handed, employs irony to distance the reader from
its subject. Since 1940, instead of structuring whole poems
from a defined point of view, Auden has tended to suggest the wider vision less obtrusively. In "Vespers" (1955)
when he is ready to speak from the broad perspective
that subsumes the philosophies of both the Arcadian and
the Utopian, he casually remarks: "Was it (as it must
look to any god of cross-roads) simply a fortuitous intersection of life-paths, loyal to different fibs [?]"[34] Even in
such cases, where it merely indicates how a few lines are
to be taken, Auden's control over point of view is clearly
aimed at lifting the reader out of himself to grasp the
general case.

The same intention directs much of his use of rhetoric.
Auden, we recall, originally described allegory as a form
of rhetoric, and he has appropriated a large number of
rhetorical constructions to assist his allegory. One of the
favorites of his early style was to suppress the article before nouns, with the effect of generalizing the significance
of the particular image. This device is well exemplified
in "1929" (1930):

> But thinking so I came at once
> Where solitary man sat weeping on a bench,

[33] *Nones* (New York, 1951), 39.
[34] *The Shield of Achilles*, 79.

> Hanging his head down, with his mouth distorted
> Helpless and ugly as an embryo chicken.[35]

The simple suppression of the indefinite article has expanded this already striking image into a figure for the whole human condition.

In more recent years Auden has used capitalization to accomplish the same generalizing aim. Sometimes his capitalizations after 1940 seem to indicate divine or absolute status, as in "The Hidden Law" of "Aera sub Lege" (1941). More consistently, capitalization simply serves to elevate a phrase to the status of a general or universal principle. In *For the Time Being* (1944), the fourth of Caesar's seven kingdoms is that of Credit Exchange:

> Instead of heavy treasures, there are paper
>   symbols of value;
> Instead of Pay at Once, there is Pay when you
>   can;
> Instead of My Neighbour, there is Our Cus-
>   tomers;
> Instead of Country Fair, there is World Market.
> Great is Caesar: God must be with Him.[36]

Each commercial commonplace is transformed into an immutable law by the capitalization, though in the case of "Our Customers" the intended abstract meaning is given additional emphasis by the use of a singular verb.

Occasionally, as with "Always" and "Never" quoted earlier from "Do Be Careful" (1930), capitalization is combined with the use of an adverb as a noun. Auden could have learned both generalizing devices from Milton, though they have become common in much modern

[35] *CP*, 62-63.
[36] *CP*, 433.

verse. "The History of Truth" (1960) is strikingly reminiscent of E. E. Cummings:

> In that ago when being was believing,
> Truth was the most of many credibles,
> More first, more always, than a bat-winged lion,
>
> . . . .
>
> Our last to do by is an anti-model,
> Some untruth anyone can give the lie to,
> A nothing no one need believe is there.[37]

The effectiveness of this device depends on its ability to
startle the reader into greater attentiveness and to direct
that attention to the general concept that is not stated
directly.

The most pervasive rhetorical figure in Auden's poetry
is personification. Clearly this device serves a dramatic
function as well as an allegorical one, but its importance
in the present context lies in the clear distinction it creates between abstract entities. The deadly sins parade in
"Which Side Am I Supposed to Be On?" (1932): "Fear/
That laconic war-bitten captain" stands beside "Wrath
who has learnt every trick of guerrilla warfare," "Envy
their brilliant pamphleteer," and "Lust/ With his sap-
per's skill."[38] More often Auden is interested in isolating
human emotions, like the "despair with hardened eye-
balls" of "Family Ghosts" (1930), or psychic faculties
like the human intellect personified in Malin in *The Age
of Anxiety* (1947). Similarly, Auden appropriates mythological figures as personifications of philosophical principles. Aphrodite and Dame Kind are prominent representations of the sensual life in the poems of the 1950's,

[37] *Homage to Clio*, 65.
[38] *CP*, 138.

[85]

just as Eros frequently was in the preceding decade.[39] In his Harvard Phi Beta Kappa poem of 1946, "Under Which Lyre" (1951), Auden develops two opposing philosophical attitudes toward the postwar world, attaching them to the figures of Apollo and Hermes.

The same poem can illustrate another allegorizing technique: the list. Instead of offering a single image to make the abstract concrete, the poet offers a list of examples in order to keep the reader from locating a poem's meaning in any single image; by this common traditional tactic he forces the reader to grasp the general principle which provides the only relatedness of the items on the list. In "Under Which Lyre," Auden endorses a "Hermetic Decalogue," which concludes as follows:

> Thou shalt not be on friendly terms
> With guys in advertising firms,
>   Nor speak with such
> As read the Bible for its prose,
> Nor, above all, make love to those
>   Who wash too much.
>
> Thou shalt not live within thy means
> Nor on plain water and raw greens.
>   If you must choose
> Between the chances, choose the odd;
> Read *The New Yorker*, trust in God;
>   And take short views.[40]

[39] One of Auden's remarks on medieval allegory may be helpful in dealing with his own use of mythological figures: "If an emotion or a concept is thought of as being absolute or given, that is, as being its own cause for being, then it may be represented as an immortal god or goddess." "Introduction" to *Poets of the English Language*, vol. 1, xxiv.

[40] *Nones*, 70. The last two phrases incorporate Auden's favorite quotation from Sydney Smith. The list of examples has one poten-

The incongruous jumble of religiously serious principles and apparent trivia helps to create the sense that Hermes stands for an all-embracing outlook on life. Thus, again, the reader is driven away from any one particular toward the general meaning.

In one of his descriptions of allegory Auden asserted that metaphor is a form of allegory (see note 22 above). Terminology is difficult, but, employing more or less traditional conceptions of these terms, his comment would seem to apply not to metaphor as a simple rhetorical figure, but to extended metaphor as a constructional device. In allegory physical resemblance between the abstract meaning and the particular that signifies it is not essential.[41] What is important is that one palpable set of images comes to stand for another which is less palpable. Ordinarily a metaphor, considered as an implied comparison, relies largely on physical similarities between the terms of the comparison, as in Coleridge's "the copper sun." An extended metaphor, however, may be considered a form of allegory when one of the terms of comparison is so abstract as to lack physical qualities. Auden has written a number of poems of this type; one is "It's So Dull Here" (1936), which begins, "To settle in this village of the heart,/ My darling, can you bear it?"[42] The terms of comparison are set immediately, and the reader

---

tial aesthetic drawback: once begun, it contains no inherent reason for stopping at any particular length, i.e., the poet's imagination is put on its mettle. Much of Auden's revising of earlier poems for the *Collected Poetry* took the form of eliminating excessive examples. Most revised poems, like "Danse Macabre" (1940), for example, are stronger for the surgery.

[41] See *DH*, 301-302, where Auden develops this traditional distinction.

[42] *CP*, 144.

understands the remaining images of village life as direct signs for the condition of the speaker's heart. The poet is interested not in the comparison, but in the impalpable entities that constitute the state of the heart.

Into the same category fall a large number of poems in the particular allegorical genre that Auden has developed most—the allegorized landscape, or, as he titles it in one poem, "Paysage Moralisé." He gives the credit for creating this genre to Rilke, who was, to Auden, the first poet since the seventeenth century to find a fresh way of concretizing the abstract. One of his characteristic devices was this same "expression of human life in terms of landscape."[43] In more recent years Auden has also praised Dante because he "endows states of mind with the urgency of places. Despair, for instance, becomes a burning plain; repentance, a green lawn."[44] A landscape is particularly useful for Auden since its landmarks are logically imagined as separate entities and are by nature arranged in some scheme. He can easily identify some feature of the landscape with an abstraction. Most often he projects onto the landscape an arrangement of human faculties, as we have seen in "Have a Good Time," or differing human philosophies, as in "In Praise of Limestone" (1951).

Auden has found the schematized allegorical landscape such an intriguing device that he has carried it on to conceive a moralized civilization.

I have devised a cultural-psychological test which I am seriously thinking of patenting. This takes the form of

[43] "Rilke in English," *The New Republic*, c (September 6, 1939), 135.

[44] "Conversation on Cornelia Street V," *Accent*, XIII (Winter 1953), 46.

a questionnaire about the subject's conception of Eden, his Innocent Place where no contradiction has yet arisen between the demands of Pleasure and the demands of Duty. What is its landscape, the ethnic origin of its inhabitants, its religion, its form of state, its architecture, its system of weights and measures, et cetera.[45]

Such cultural manifestations have provided effective imagery for a number of poems. "Vespers," as we saw in the preceding chapter, studies the moral and religious significance of their citizenship to an Arcadian and a Utopian. The poem contrasts their reactions to sharply particular cultural signs like lights burning late in the police station and ugly lampshades in shop windows. The seven "Bucolics," also in *The Shield of Achilles*, are essentially Auden's commentary on the kinds of people who would have lakes, mountains, and so on, as their ideal Innocent Places. Also the nature of the countryside can project the general condition of a civilization. The landscape of rusting machinery and abandoned mines so prevalent in his early verse reveals "a lot about a country's soul," just as "The trees encountered on a country stroll"[46] do in 1955. Even the points of the compass are moralized. "North must seem the 'good' direction, the way towards heroic adventures, South the way to ignoble ease and decadence."[47] The map is a related allegorical image for a person's private picture of the way the land lies as opposed to the actual terrain. Hence, in 1937, Auden counsels the dejected lover to "Stand up and

[45] "England: Six Unexpected Days," *Vogue*, cxxiii (May 15, 1954), 62. Recently Auden has completed his own questionnaire, *DH*, 6-7.
[46] *The Shield of Achilles*, 15.
[47] "England," 62. See also "Good-bye to the Mezzogiorno" (1960), in *Homage to Clio*.

fold/ Your map of desolation."[48] In a poem like "Musée des Beaux Arts" (1940) Auden can even invade the landscape in a painting, in this case Breughel's *Icarus*, to isolate the moral point. Indeed, Auden quite frankly admits that "what interests me most about a painting is its iconography."[49]

There seems to be no imagery that Auden cannot turn to an allegorical use. He himself recommends as part of the curriculum of an ideal Bardic College "courses in mathematics, natural history, geology, meteorology, archaeology, mythology, liturgics and cooking."[50] Moreover, he introduces material from all these fields into his poetry whenever it will provide strikingly apt imagery for illustrating or embodying his schematic analysis. Indeed, except in a few of his earliest Georgian poems and a few in his 1960 volume, nearly every image, be it from a landscape or mathematics, is moralized or humanized.

We have considered Auden's habitual use of allegory as a technique by which he can bring the private into contact with the public. Allegory, with its reliance on the intellectual and rational, focuses poetic attention on general ideas which can apply to a wide group of human individuals and, in that sense, achieve public status. The particular images that make the abstract point palpable are present not because they have autobiographical importance, but because they assist in making the general point available to the reader. Auden's attempt is to re-establish, by allegorical means, the relation between the

[48] *CP*, 232.

[49] "The Problem of Nowness," *The Mid-Century*, No. 19 (November 1960), 14.

[50] "The Poet as Professor," *The* [London] *Observer Weekend Review* (January 5, 1961), 21. *DH*, 77.

personal and the public which has been lost to so many in the modern world.

Since Auden refuses to be satisfied with a Romantic retreat into the purely personal and subjective, he has been alert to other means of turning outward besides allegory. He found in the occasional poems of William Butler Yeats a useful precedent. Auden seems to have "discovered" Yeats in the middle 1930's. By 1937, he was quoting Yeats in reference to himself, apparently describing the newly reinforced challenge he felt in attempting to write poetry in complex and demanding stanza forms. Indeed, "the fascination of what's difficult" has seemed to move Auden as much as Yeats.[51] One of the main legacies Yeats left to Auden was occasional poetry, like "In Memory of Major Robert Gregory." As Auden puts it in one of his tributes to Yeats: "He transformed a certain kind of poem, the occasional poem, from being either an official performance of impersonal virtuosity or a trivial *vers de société* into a serious reflective poem of at once personal and public interest."[52] In Auden's 1940 volume, *Another Time,* there appeared for the first time a section entitled "Occasional Poems." Since then a substantial number of his poems have taken their subjects from some publicly important personage or event, ranging from the anniversary of the Crucifixion to that of Mozart's birth.

The value of the occasional poem for Auden is that it provides him with a noteworthy historical personage or event, usually outside his direct personal experience, through which he can imply or project a universal significance. When he succeeds, to use Auden's own word,

[51] See "A Letter to Lord Byron," *Letters from Iceland,* 22.
[52] "Yeats as an Example," *Kenyon Review,* x (Spring 1948), 193.

the occasion has "resonance."[53] The poet himself does not postulate direct personal relation to the occasional subject; rather, he acquires a relation to this public phenomenon by perceiving and developing its general or universal significance. The same can be true for the reading audience, for the poet calls attention to nothing that is private or dependent on his personal experience. The occasion is treated objectively, employing only those details about it which would be available to anyone turning his attention in that direction. As in the case of Auden's allegory, this objective, impersonal approach to the subject ends by giving both reader and poet a sense of relatedness to the particular occasion through their association with its universalized significance.

Since Auden's "In Memory of W. B. Yeats" is itself his most brilliant performance in this genre, a brief commentary may clarify its use. From the start the poet asserts no particular personal loss in the death of Yeats; at most, he may be among the "few thousand" who "will think of this day/ As one thinks of a day when one did something slightly unusual." In fact, the painful insistence of the poem is that this death has had and apparently can have little effect on the world. Robert Roth points out that Auden's means for developing the poem are "anti-hyperbolic." The whole poem is a "conscious controversion" of the traditional consolations of the pastoral elegy.[54] Nature is totally unaffected; its only reaction to Yeats's last day is recorded by impersonal weather instruments. It is purely coincidence that "The day of his

[53] "Foreword," to W. S. Merwin, A *Mask for Janus* (New Haven, 1952), vii.
[54] "The Sophistication of W. H. Auden," *Modern Philology*, XLVIII (February 1951), 199.

death was a dark cold day." The social world, with the exception of the few thousand whose lives are slightly affected, remains the same: "the poor have the sufferings to which they are fairly accustomed." The dead man himself, far from being ennobled by the poem, is described as "silly like us." Even his poetry cannot stand as a monument, for "The words of a dead man/ Are modified in the guts of the living." The initial sections of the poem deny that personal lives have impact on the world. This death and the life that preceded it seem fruitless, for each man still lives in "the cell of himself." The anti-Romantic debunking of traditional eulogy offers a hard comfort to the reader. The projected view of human life insists on very limited possibilities for human accomplishment. However, the reader is led to assent at least to the rigid honesty and accuracy of the poem's assessment. Through the medium of that assent Auden develops the universal significance of the death of Yeats, which is by implication the death of any poet, if not of any man. Despite the fact that "poetry makes nothing happen," "Time . . . worships language and forgives/ Everyone by whom it lives." In effect, Auden is saying that though poets may die, language lives on, and the significance of the life of language is made clear in the final three stanzas:

> Follow, poet, follow right
> To the bottom of the night,
> With your unconstraining voice
> Still persuade us to rejoice;
>
> With the farming of a verse
> Make a vineyard of the curse,
> Sing of human unsuccess
> In a rapture of distress;

[93]

In the deserts of the heart
Let the healing fountain start,
In the prison of his days
Teach the free man how to praise.[55]

After insisting that all men are actually trapped in a prison of limitations, Auden here affirms that the poet has accomplished one thing—he has made it conceivable that men might freely choose to praise the life that they have. Once this universal significance of language and its poetic use has been accepted, it constitutes the value of poetry and consolation for the death of a poet. The reader may be moved to feel personal gratitude for Yeats, whose poetry has been one of the particular agents helping human beings to recognize and rejoice in the true terms of their existence. At least Auden, in this poem, has created a credible justification for such gratitude.

Thus, the way in which Auden employs the occasional poem to establish a relation between the personal and the public is closely analogous to his use of allegory. In this century the poet and his audience rarely feel direct personal relatedness to the larger public world. For most the parallel connection between particular and Universal or Absolute is also severed. Yet the particular, be it a human individual or an experimental datum, only gains significance by its location in a larger world. To counter these discontinuities Auden's poetry has relied on anti-Romantic techniques that suppress the privately subjective and affirm the priority of the supra-personal and the rational. Poetic particulars are important only as they can illustrate or stand for a generally applicable insight or truth. By hard-headed analysis of the human situation

[55] CP, 51.

and the generalizing devices of rhetoric and allegory, Auden leads the reader toward recognizing a larger scheme of things in which he may have a personal place. The resulting poetry relies heavily on intellect in its construction and hence it demands a "thought-full" response. Those with Romantic expectations may find the poetry distant and unfeeling at first contact. Auden, however, hopes that an understanding of the general and abstract can serve as one step toward a renewed feeling for and contact with other individuals in the world. Men feel isolated from each other partly because they fail to recognize overarching general truths to which all men are subject. Metaphorically speaking, we are all in a circus tent called the human situation. Recognizing truths about our common humanness can make us more responsive to the individuals sitting around us and to the performer in the ring, whose name might be Yeats, or even Auden. In religious terms one might state the case analogously: through a sense of the Divine, of what is beyond the human, one can come for the first time to love one's neighbor. This process, as so often with Auden, is highly indirect, but it does propose a reasonable poetic means for coping with the modern sense of isolated subjectivity.

CHAPTER IV

DRAMATIC INDIRECTIONS

THE traditional means for vitalizing abstract allegorical poems include the use of a dramatic framework to arrange an immediate confrontation between differing ideas or points of view. Throughout his work Auden has created such dramatic structuring wherever possible. We obviously encounter dramatic poetry in the three plays he wrote with Christopher Isherwood and opera libretti like *The Rake's Progress* (1951) with Chester Kallman. A second group, less strictly dramatic, includes most of Auden's other long works from the charade, "Paid on Both Sides" (1930), to his most recent long poem, *The Age of Anxiety* (1947). We might call them "semi-dramas" or, perhaps, "lectern dramas." Though they are best suited to reading, their format presumes at least the dramatic convention of characters speaking in dialogue.[1]

In the third and least formally dramatic group, most of them shorter poems, Auden creates an "implied drama." The speaker may offer a prayer, compose a letter, or deliver an oration to a presumed audience; opposite or conflicting solutions to a problem may be projected into two personifying characters; or, especially in his earlier works, Auden may present a dramatic monologue where a mind is divided against itself. Even in an occasional poem like "Musée des Beaux Arts" (1940), which studies the place of suffering in life, Auden makes his point by taking the

---

[1] The most obvious exception among the long poems is "New Year Letter" (1941), which is a rational discourse in verse. Even in such a setting, however, Auden cannot resist having the Devil dramatize his temptations in a long set speech.

reader with him into the dramatic situation of Breughel's *Icarus*.

Auden's instincts consistently lead him to project poems in some sort of dramatic frame, however vague and unsatisfactory the drama might be from the strict point of view of the stage. Such extensive use of dramatic devices is no surprise in the work of an anti-Romantic poet, for at least one logical alternative to personal self-expression is an indirect dramatic presentation. In judging the poems of others, Auden demands that a poet be "interested in something more than his precious little self."[2] He has asked the same of himself from the start.

While Auden's reader finds dramatic devices everywhere, he encounters little "drama" in the Aristotelian sense, and no dramaturgy. Auden characteristically presents the conventional trappings of drama without the traditional development of character and conflict. His mode involves another sort of drama that is abstract and allegorical rather than naturalistic. As Monroe Spears remarks, even the plays Auden and Isherwood wrote for the stage are "fables, modern morality plays; they are intended to appeal to the minds and not the emotions of the audience."[3]

Auden's inclination toward a highly structured and relatively static drama is implicit in his attraction to John Skelton's *Magnificence*. As early as 1932 he finds this interlude "an excellent acting play."[4] Again in 1935 he praises Skelton's success in differentiating characters by making them speak in different metres. He suggests that

[2] "Foreword," to William Dickey, *Of the Festivity* (New Haven, 1959), ix-x.
[3] *Poetry of Auden*, 91.
[4] Review of *The Complete Works of John Skelton*, ed. Philip Henderson, *Criterion*, XI (January 1932), 318.

"for the future of poetic comedy it may prove important."[5]
While Auden did not rely on Skelton's devices wholly or
with great success until semi-dramas like "The Sea and
the Mirror" (1944), his plays with Isherwood clearly indicate his commitment to such formal structure. The
characters are personified attitudes of mind more than
recognizably particular human individuals, and the author
develops contrasts between them rather than conflict. The
dramatic interest is not centered in plot, because the characters are presented without a personal history and largely
without development. Instead of cumulative interaction,
the plays concentrate on defining static relationships. In
The Ascent of F6 (1936), for example, the attitude of
the average man, embodied in Mr. and Mrs. A, contrasts
with the attitude of the strong leader, Michael Ransom.
There is neither contact nor conflict between them, though
both appear on stage at the same time. They represent
two mutually exclusive ways of life that have only occasional and distant influence on each other. As we have
seen in relation to Auden's penchant for allegory, he has
always been more interested in states of being than in
individuals. Given this initial impulse toward the abstract
and general, Auden can use even a vaguely dramatic context to make abstractions more palpable than they would
otherwise be.

As usual, Auden has been aware of his inclinations, and
he has judged them a limitation. His own inability to
create unique and individual characters lies behind his
often noted admiration for the art of the novelist, who
must do so or debilitate his work. Auden concludes that
the interest of D. H. Lawrence in states of being was "a

[5] "John Skelton," in *The Great Tudors*, ed. Katharine Garvin
(New York, 1935), 67.

serious drawback in writing fiction which cannot avoid the individual and his relations to other individuals over a stretch of time."[6] Again, in reviewing William Plomer's poems, Auden compares the two genres in similar terms: "A good novelist must also be a potential poet, but a good poet need not also be a potential novelist . . . [because] good poetry can be written without any feeling for character."[7]

Before we survey Auden's semi-dramas and the shorter poems with implied drama, a closer study of his explicitly dramatic works can demonstrate most clearly his limited type of drama. His plays, as John Bradbury observes, are "dramatic without being drama."[8] The formal and abstract elements of drama are strikingly prominent in the theory he outlines to justify his practice in the plays:

> The development of the film has deprived drama of any excuse for being documentary. . . .
>
> The drama is not suited to analysis of character, which is the province of the novel. Dramatic characters are simplified, easily recognizable and over life-size. . . .
>
> Drama in fact deals with the general and universal, not with the particular and local.[9]

In performance the dramatic weakness in Auden's theory becomes most obvious. *The Ascent of F6* is, from the

---

[6] "Some Notes on D. H. Lawrence," 482.

[7] "A Novelist's Poems," *Poetry* [Chicago], XLIX (January 1937), 223. Auden was a guest editor for this issue. See also "The Novelist" (1940), *CP*, 39, and *Letters from Iceland*, 20, for similar comparisons belittling the poet.

[8] "Auden and the Tradition," *Western Review*, XII (Summer 1948), 229.

[9] From "What I Want the Theatre to Be," printed in the program of the Group Theatre production of *The Dance of Death* and *Sweeney Agonistes*, Autumn 1935, as quoted in Ashley Dukes, "The English Scene," *Theatre Arts*, XIX (December 1935), 907-908.

point of view of the stage, his most successful play because in Michael Ransom he comes closest to creating a viable stage character. But even here the characters of Mr. and Mrs. A are such "simplified" and "easily recognizable" types as to make their physical embodiment in the actors seem absurd. They are so completely abstractions of the average frustrated couple and so little like whole human beings that they are better heard than seen. In other words, Auden succeeds dramatically when he goes beyond "the general and universal," when he violates his own theoretical understanding of the true dramatic matrix—which may be no more than to admit that the stage makes its own demands.

Michael Ransom, accordingly, is worthy of particular attention: he is the one character who comes close to being a specific individual with a specific history. Even so, he neither generates nor participates in the kind of cumulative interaction characteristic of the naturalistic play. He is a typological character involved primarily in a succession of static relationships with others. A study in one of Auden's favorite type-figures, Michael is the "truly strong" man. His prototype appears in poems around 1930 as "The tall unwounded leader/ Of doomed companions."[10] He re-emerges as a shadowy leader-savior in *The Orators*, referred to only as "Him." In *F6* Michael's mother reveals that she had denied her love to him so that he might become totally self-sufficient: "You were to be the truly strong/ Who must be kept from all that could infect/ Or weaken."[11] His stature in relation to the other characters is implied through schematic staging. In one

[10] See "Missing," *CP*, 43.
[11] *The Ascent of F6* (New York, 1937), 45. More readily available in *Two Great Plays*, Modern Library paperback (New York, n.d.), 138.

stage box sit Mr. and Mrs. A, the obviously weak; in another on the opposite side sit the apparently strong characters, such as James Ransom and Lord Stagmantle. Possessed of worldly power, these figures nevertheless require flattery and admiration to keep their strength. Dominating center stage are Michael and his motley group of climbers.

Michael's strength in relation to his own group is dramatized in his ability to reconcile opposites, a necessary characteristic of the truly strong man. Auden has never respected simple-minded revolt as a means of solving a problem. As he put it in 1930: "Yours you say were parents to avoid, avoid them if you please/ Do the reverse on all occasions till you catch the same disease."[12] In Auden's eyes, the truest strength lies in the ability to rise above simple opposition to a higher synthesis. Michael Ransom, to be strong, must resist the temptation to negate everything his twin brother James does and is. Early in the play we learn that Michael is an uncompromising idealist, whose fondest dream is to lead the first attempt to climb F6. His temptation arises when his politician brother offers government support for an expedition when F6 suddenly becomes a focal point of international competition for colonial power. Michael is inclined to refuse for the sake of frustrating his brother and the worldly power James represents. Also, Michael realizes that to agree would be to do the right thing for the wrong reasons. Finally, under pressure from his mother, he accepts, hoping his own motives are pure enough to keep the expedition free from taint.

Ultimately Michael fails, but his temporary success is projected dramatically in his handling of the climbers under him. The neuroses of two of his men are in direct

[12] *Poems* (1930), XXII, 40. Not reprinted in *CP*.

opposition to each other: David Gunn, the overly frivolous kleptomaniac, is the anti-type of overly serious and proper Ian Shawcross. Through most of the play Michael is strong enough to hold these opposites in balance so that both men can contribute to the expedition. Later, the gradual destruction of the group of climbers mirrors the progressive disintegration within Michael.

The schematic structure of the play becomes explicit in Act II, Scene 5, after the narrative proper has ended with Michael's collapse near the summit of the mountain. The play ends with a series of set pieces in the form of tableaux, which ostensibly we are to take as the passing dumb show of Michael's subconscious mind as he nears death. There is a chess game between James and Michael Ransom, with the other characters as pieces, and a burlesque court scene held to judge both brothers. Finally appearing on the summit of the mountain, Michael lays his head in the lap of a veiled figure; she is disclosed as his mother, his personal daemon. In these final scenes the characters lose whatever dramatic reality they have attained and become abstractions. Michael is revealed as a superficially strong man who failed to be "truly strong," a man driven by a hyper-acute Oedipus complex to conceive himself as a heroic world-savior. James and his cohorts are the world's rulers who gain a hollow power by reconciling the average, Mr. and Mrs. A, to the lot that life offers them.

This schematic construction in the last scenes of *F6* may be seen in Auden's other plays. *On the Frontier* and especially *The Dog Beneath the Skin* move from one set piece to another with little dramatic motivation. The movement of the latter play resembles not a movie film but a series of slides. When Alan Norman travels around Europe in search of the missing heir, there is no discernible dramatic logic to the succession of scenes he witnesses. Individually, many sections sparkle with inventive satiric wit, and they may still be read with pleasure, but collectively their worth as stagecraft is dubious. As a group they are intended to portray the political and psychological state of Europe at the time, but their order seems arbitrary. Only the thinnest thread connects the scenes: Alan must travel on to some other place if he is to continue the search for Francis. The play is, in effect, a succession of tableaux without adequate interrelation or logical sequence.

Looseness of dramatic links between self-contained scenes makes it easy for Auden to extract sections from these plays and reprint them separately. One extraction is of particular critical interest because Joseph Warren Beach chose it as major evidence for his contention that Auden as a poet lacks "integrality." In the Vicar's sermon from *The Dog Beneath the Skin,* the orator works himself into a frenzy calling for a holy war against Bolshevism and the Devil. The context of the play makes it clear that the Vicar, like the speaker of "Danse Macabre," is one of Auden's demonic prophets, self-called to God to eradicate the Mistaken from the earth. In his *Collected Poetry* he reprinted the prose piece, virtually without change, as "Depravity: A Sermon." Accompanying this appearance was a preliminary note expressing the hope that the sermon would seem meaningless to those who were not professing Christians. Beach is dismayed at what he sees as Auden's use of the same satirical piece to imply two opposite attitudes toward religion. His objection is both aesthetic and religious.

Despite his attempts to be fair to Auden the reconverted Christian, Beach fails to overcome fully the bias of his own rational humanism. His remark on the Vicar's sermon, "We don't see how the same elaborate work can serve both God and Mammon,"[13] makes an oversimple distinction. He assumes that as an attack on corruption in the clergy, it must serve Mammon. By the same argument even *Piers Plowman* would be labelled as anti-religious. A believer, whether clergyman or layman, should feel the need to recognize corruptions of his religion in himself and others, to the end that he might better abide by his faith. Even the original context of the play emphasizes that Auden is satirizing corruption in the clergy, not the clergy itself. The Curate, though weak-willed, is a churchman who recognizes the evil in the Vicar's words.

More important, however, is Beach's aesthetic objection. He assumes that a poem is a verbal structure which can have only one basic meaning, since it is an organic self-expression of the poet. Auden, however, removes the poem from its original setting into an entirely unrelated context. He must, in Beach's view, have been badly confused to think that the same verbal structure could, without being changed, serve another than its original "intention."[14] Yet one can see that Auden's practice takes into account an important fact about the nature of

[13] *Auden Canon*, 249.

[14] See *Auden Canon*, 180, for example. In the case of individual lines Auden has similarly re-used earlier material. In *Poetry of Auden* Monroe Spears calls attention to later use of several lines which first appeared in *Poems* (1928). In a startling instance from Auden's prose, we find him adapting the same aphoristic quip to differing contexts four times from 1934 to 1962. In *DH* (p. 14) it is used to mock the social worker out of his own mouth: "We are all here on earth to help others; what on earth the others are here for, I don't know." But see also, *Oxford and the Groups*, ed. Richard Crossman (Oxford, 1934), 90-91; "Squares and Oblongs," (1948), 177; "Charles Williams," *Christian Century*, LXXIII (May 2, 1956), 552.

words—what they mean depends to a considerable extent on the context in which they are received. In reprinting the Vicar's sermon, what Auden did change was the angle from which he wanted the reader to approach the sermon. Apparently Beach was unaware that Auden had treated his "original" intention with equal irreverence once before. The same piece appeared originally in 1934 as "Sermon by an Armaments Manufacturer."[15] In this first printing the title frames still another context in which the poem may be read—a context which points the satire at capitalism.

The crucial difference in thinking here is that, whereas a neo-Romantic critic locates the substance of the poem in the poet's self-expression, Auden treats the poem as a performance. He examines the poem from the audience's point of view; he controls its implications by means of the context in which he presents it.

That Auden could so easily extract the Vicar's sermon as a self-contained set piece is, however, some evidence of the weakness of his plays as connected stagecraft. Auden is always writing parables which transform a particular occasion into a poem. Then if some new work involves an analogous occasion, the original poem can function in the context of a different mosaic. Auden commonly treats his long works as if they were stage scenery whose sections might be, and sometimes are, dismantled at will and rearranged for use before another audience. The effectiveness of the new composite, however, depends on its ability to establish a larger frame of reference which relates the individual set pieces to each other. In addition, if it is a play, the new work must develop a coherent progression of scenes whose unity can be made manifest by

[15] *Life and Letters*, x (May 1934), 164-167.

the actors on stage. Too often in Auden's plays the self-sufficient sections fail to achieve coherence of a dramatic kind. At best, they are structural equivalents, in a lower key, of Goethe's *Faust*, which is, of course, much like opera. And like *Faust*, their primary impact is not dramatic, but philosophic. Since 1940 Auden has limited his writing for stage production to operas. This redirection of his energies seems wise in the light of his particular propensities as a playwright. Characteristics of Auden's drama which are limitations in a play can make a positive contribution to a libretto. In opera the dramaturgy must necessarily be broken into set pieces to allow for arias and ensembles. The genre demands that characters be larger than life-size, and the music contributes the emotional immediacy often lacking in Auden's plays. Although the plays are little more than interesting experiments, *The Rake's Progress* (analyzed in Chapter 6) is surely one of the best libretti written in this century and among Auden's stage works the best suited to the requirements of its genre.

Auden's semi-dramas—longer works which assume stage conventions but are intended primarily for reading—fall somewhere between drama and Platonic dialogue in form. These are generally more successful than his plays. Since the characters are divorced from visually arranged particulars of space and time, from surroundings or locality, the reader is less likely to be disturbed by their lack of sharp individuality. Similarly, the reader can more easily accommodate the changes in perspective that Auden demands. The semi-drama form also projects the poem in a self-sufficient form clearly divorced from the author as speaker. However shadowy the dramatic situation may be, it still helps objectify the abstract point. Even vague characters can help the reader locate the various philosophical attitudes that may be placed in relation to each other by the poem.

The semi-drama with its quasi-dramatic characters and situation has stimulated some of Auden's finest poetry. "The Sea and the Mirror" can serve as an example of his practice at its best. This particular poem is especially significant since it yields a partial explanation for his experimenting with the semi-drama in the first place.

As is usual in Auden's plays, "The Sea and the Mirror" is constructed from nearly autonomous set pieces, but here they participate in a brilliantly unified whole. As Edward Callan suggests in the most penetrating analysis of the poem yet written, they are composed into a triptych with the three compartments or panels focusing in turn on the artist, the work of art, and the audience.[16] The metaphor of the triptych is highly appropriate to suggest the elegant formal structure of this work. Within the tripartite framework, the differentiating verse forms assigned to each character give the kind of formal unity in diversity Auden earlier admired in Skelton's *Magnificence*. He succeeds in individualizing each personality in an appropriate form, many of them notably intricate and demanding. With two minor exceptions, all the characters come from Shakespeare's *The Tempest*, though Auden feels free to treat them as types that are of particular in-

[16] See the unpublished dissertation (University of South Africa, Pretoria, 1958), "A Study of the Relationship of Structure and Meaning in W. H. Auden's Major Poems, 1940-1955," 95 ff., to which the following discussion is much indebted. See Callan, "Auden's Ironic Masquerade: Criticism as Morality Play," forthcoming in *University of Toronto Quarterly*. The triptych metaphor is briefly developed in Callan's "Auden's *New Year Letter*: A New Style of Architecture," *Renascence*, XVI (Fall 1963), 18-19. Reprinted in *Auden*, ed. Monroe K. Spears, 159.

terest to him.[17] *The Tempest* provides Auden with a widely known situation that can help particularize the terms of his own analysis; it also frees him from the necessity of developing his own specific characters. If Auden's use of Shakespeare makes "The Sea and the Mirror" less than self-sufficient as a work of art, the price for such brilliance is small.

Ostensibly the drama begins after Shakespeare's epilogue to *The Tempest* has raised serious questions about the nature of art. Its subject is the relation between the sea and the mirror, between the actual world and the hypothetical world called art. The first is bound by life and death; the second is outside of time and infinitely variable. There is no action and the poem takes place in no space. Only earthy Caliban suggests that he is standing in front of a theater curtain.

The first compartment is devoted to the artist, Prospero, who is finally releasing his imagination, Ariel. While maintaining the general situation of Prospero at the end of *The Tempest*, Auden pointedly has this Prospero describe his situation in words that might come from any artist—Shakespeare or, perhaps, Auden—who encounters the ultimate limitation of his art. He knows now that it can never substitute for life (the sea). Ignoring the particular circumstances of his exile from Milan, Prospero describes his initial practice of art as magic in terms reminiscent of Freud:

> When I woke into my life, a sobbing dwarf
> Whom giants served only as they pleased, I was not
> what I seemed;

[17] The two exceptions are the Stage Manager, who speaks a preface to the critics, and the Prompter, who contributes an echo to Ariel's postscript.

Beyond their busy backs I made a magic
To ride away from a father's imperfect justice,
    Take vengeance on the Romans for their
        grammar,
Usurp the popular earth and blot out forever
    The gross insult of being a mere one among
        many:
Now, Ariel, I am that I am, your late and lonely
    master,
    Who knows now what magic is:—the power to
      enchant
That comes from disillusion.[18]

The master of the power to enchant can see himself clearly only when he gives up his dependence on the Ariel of the imagination. Heretofore Ariel has been kept busy magically remaking the real world to conform to his master's idea of the way things should be. Now Prospero sees what the freely acting imagination can show him: "All we are not stares back at what we are." Living on without his familiar imagination is bound to be hard. He wonders, "Can I learn to suffer/ Without saying something ironic or funny/ On suffering?" Ultimately, of course, he must do so, for the artist, like all men, must reconcile himself to "a universe where time is not foreshortened,/ No animals talk, and there is neither floating nor flying."

The second compartment of the triptych, representing the work of art, introduces the remaining characters from *The Tempest* except for Caliban. They reveal the results of Prospero's last acts of magic. He had suggested in the first section that "The extravagant children, who lately

[18] CP, 353-354. For a parallel analysis based on Freud, see "Art and Psychology," in *The Arts Today*, ed. G. Grigson (London, 1935), esp. p. 6.

swaggered/ Out of the sea like gods, have, I think, been soundly hunted/ By their own devils into their human selves." In other words, after having presumed that they could transform the circumstances of their lives, these characters are once again reconciled to the sea of life, where each must live within his particular human limitations.

The verse sections in this second compartment are dazzling in their virtuosity, for Auden has risen to meet his stringent, self-imposed demands. Each character expresses the conditions of his reconciliation to his human self in diction and on a level of thinking that is appropriate to the form in which the poem is cast, and both matter and manner are fitted to the character who is speaking. Ferdinand expresses his love for Miranda in a sonnet; she returns hers in a delicate villanelle; Sebastian voices his intricate ambitions in a sestina, while the sailors and Trinculo lament in different types of ballad. Stephano ironically woos his belly in a ballade. Gonzalo and Alonso speak in complex and dignified forms of Auden's own invention. Antonio proclaims his commitment to perversity in terza rima. The short poem given to the Master and Boatswain can serve as an example of the concentration and aptness of the poetry in this section. Their poem uses a six-line stanza composed of a ballad quatrain plus an added couplet. Stephano's song from *The Tempest* (ii, ii) provides the raw material that Auden develops with deft appropriateness:

> At Dirty Dick's and Sloppy Joe's
>   We drank our liquor straight,
> Some went upstairs with Margery,
>   And some, alas, with Kate;

And two by two like cat and mouse
The homeless played at keeping house.

There Wealthy Meg, the Sailor's Friend,
        And Marion, cow-eyed,
Opened their arms to me but I
        Refused to step inside;
I was not looking for a cage
In which to mope in my old age.

The nightingales are sobbing in
        The orchards of our mothers,
And hearts that we broke long ago
        Have long been breaking others;
Tears are round, the sea is deep:
Roll them overboard and sleep.[19]

Not only are form, setting, and diction appropriate to the characters and to each other, but also this little ballad fits neatly into the wider dramatic framework of the second section. The sailors, however joylessly, do come to terms with the life of the sea—which is also the sea of life. Finally, in and of itself the poem is powerful and moving; it is an example of Auden's most vigorous ballad style.

As is characteristic of Auden's longer works, any of these individual pieces could stand alone outside the semi-drama. They express the feelings of each character in sufficiently general terms for Auden to extract any of them as easily as he did the Vicar's sermon from *The Dog Beneath the Skin*.[20] Yet the context established by

[19] CP, 369.
[20] As if to prove the point, Auden did reprint several individual pieces from this work in his 1959 *Selected Poetry*. In the case of the Master's and Boatswain's song, Dylan Thomas also called at-

the whole series of shorter poems brings out a relatedness inherent but not explicit in the poems taken individually. The section is unified by the single theme on which each character performs his own variation—each, as Prospero has foreseen, expresses the terms of his reconciliation with his particular life situation. In Callan's words, this section constitutes "an elaborate pageant corresponding to Prospero's wedding masque in *The Tempest*."[21] As Callan goes on to show, Auden gives additional coherence to the tableau by arranging the poems to suggest a social order among the reconciled characters; Alonso appears in the center flanked by counterbalanced pairs of courtly and rustic characters.[22]

This second compartment, taken as a whole, makes particularly clear the anti-Romantic character of Auden's long poems. Stephen Spender once complained that Auden treated his work "as though a poem were not a single experience but a mosaic held together by the consistency of an atmosphere, a rhythm, or an idea common to all its parts."[23] If we except Spender's implication that a poem *ought* to be unified like "a single experience," his description of Auden's formal kind of order is valuable. When it stands alone, each set piece exhibits self-contained coherence. When several are combined, the resulting collage succeeds if it can create a higher order of unity that integrates all its constituents. The success

---

tention to its separability by reciting it with great effectiveness on his last American tour. See and hear *Dylan Thomas Reading*, vol. 4, Caedmon Recording TC 1061.

[21] Callan dissertation, 105; Callan article, 19. (See above, note 16.)

[22] Callan dissertation, 111; Callan article, 19. (See above, note 16.)

[23] "Auden and His Poetry," 75. Reprinted *Auden*, ed. Monroe K. Spears, 29.

of "The Sea and the Mirror" vindicates Auden's treatment of the poem as a performance to be repeated whenever and wherever useful.

Not only does this semi-drama exemplify Auden's anti-Romantic practices, but it also contains its own justification. Auden introduces spokesmen for the Romantic aesthetic only to reject it. Antonio, who is the only character who perversely refuses to be reconciled by Prospero's art, is the first Romantic prototype. Callan suggests that, philosophically speaking, Antonio may be the sole embodiment in Auden's poetry of his concept of the "negative religious hero," developed in *The Enchafèd Flood* and elsewhere. In aesthetic terms, however, as Callan recognizes, Antonio represents in section two the Romantic views later attributed to the audience.[24] Antonio refuses in turn each of the forms of reconciliation found by the other characters; he insists that Prospero must continue to try to charm him. In effect he serves as the overly faithful public that will not let the old master retire.

> Antonio, sweet brother, has to laugh.
> How easy you have made it to refuse
> Peace to your greatness! Break your wand in half,
>
> The fragments will join; burn your books or lose
> Them in the sea, they will soon reappear,
> Not even damaged: as long as I choose
>
> To wear my fashion, whatever you wear
> Is a magic robe; while I stand outside
> Your circle, the will to charm is still there.[25]

Most significant here are Antonio's means for disrupting Prospero's peaceful retirement. They are to tempt Prospero

[24] Callan dissertation, 109.
[25] *CP*, 360-361.

once more to practice his magical art, even though he has now outgrown his Romantic trust in the imagination as a substitute for life:

In section three, the compartment devoted primarily to the audience, Auden more explicitly demolishes the Romantic aesthetic. Caliban speaks the entire section in prose, albeit a rhetorically luxuriant prose in the later manner of Henry James. Like James's prefaces and late novels, the discourse demands total concentration on the part of the reader. While this section is, as Monroe Spears suggests, baroque in its elaboration,[26] it sparkles with polished particularity that brings its complex and abstract subject vividly to life. In essence, Auden is attempting to demonstrate the dangers of misconceiving the artistic performance. As Callan observes, Auden finds in this age a dangerous Romantic separation of art and life. If the imagined is treated as self-sufficiently real, then art becomes magic, as commonly happens in propaganda or advertising; if the imagined is taken as irrelevant to reality, then art is dismissed as merely childish play to be carried on for its own sake only.

First, the spectators, through Caliban, complain that Shakespeare's Epilogue to *The Tempest* has destroyed the pleasant illusion of the play-world, thereby, in effect, releasing Caliban into the universe of the imagination. Caliban is one of the stubbornly untransformable facts of actual existence, who, by his earthy intransigence, destroys that "perfectly tidiable case of disorder" which is the work of art. The audience insist that they are well aware that art is not life; in fact, they value art because

[26] *Poetry of Auden*, 219, 230. In my opinion Auden showed good judgment in reprinting the whole of Caliban's discourse, despite its length, in the *Selected Poetry* of 1959. This prose is as memorable as much of his poetry.

it seems to provide a totally free escape from the unpleasantness of actual life. They, like perverse Antonio in section two, insist on wanting to be charmed by the Muse:

For we, after all—you cannot have forgotten this—are strangers to her [the Muse]. We have never claimed her acquaintance, knowing as well as she that we do not and never could belong on her side of the curtain. All we have ever asked for is that for a few hours the curtain should be left undrawn, so as to allow our humble ragged selves the privilege of craning and gaping at the splendid goings-on inside.[27]

What the audience do want to insist upon is the radical division between the mirror world of art and the chaos that is life. They fear that their beloved author, who has entertained them so often, may on this occasion have done more than simply shatter the illusion of the art world. "If the intrusion of the real has disconcerted and incommoded the poetic, that is a mere bagatelle compared to the damage which the poetic would inflict if it ever succeeded in intruding on the real." The spectators fear the breakdown of the radical separateness that has kept their actual lives carefully insulated from any possibility of transformation.

Caliban, rather than answering these complaints directly, delivers a special message from the author to "any gay apprentice in the magical art who may have chosen this specimen of the prestidigitatory genus to study this evening in the hope of grasping more clearly just how the artistic contraption works." In effect, the potential artist is warned that he is subject to a temptation analogous to that of the audience. He will want to believe

[27] CP, 377-378.

that he can be the ideally imaginative Ariel to the exclusion of his grosser self, his Caliban of the body. The prospective artist must learn, as did Prospero, that he has a sea life to lead which is not "amenable to magic."

Caliban then turns to the audience at large. Speaking in the name of Shakespeare, he lauds them for having taken a first step beyond a childish identification of art and life. They are now aware of two irreconcilably different categories: the real and the imagined, Caliban with his "reiterated affirmation of what their furnished circumstances categorically are," and Ariel with "his successive propositions as to everything else they conditionally might be." Though irreconcilable, Caliban and Ariel are also interdependent. Like the two faces of Being and Becoming, they are involved in constant tension; the imagined world always measures and judges the world we actually inhabit. Human beings are endlessly tempted to avoid facing the tension by turning either to Caliban's world or to Ariel's as if one were sufficient in itself, thereby ignoring the conflict between what is and what ought to be. Such failure of moral awareness is condemned partly in aesthetic terms. If the members of the audience call Caliban, he will have no choice but to obey their foolish command to carry them back to the childish state where the ideal seemed to be embodied in the real: "Give me my passage home, let me see that harbour once again just as it was before I learned the bad words." Or if they call Ariel, they will unfailingly be transported to the state where the physically real is abandoned for the abstract ideal, that "Heaven of the Really General Case," where ideas are pure but have no material to work on. Events there "are merely elements in an allegorical landscape to which mathematical measurement and phenomenological analysis have no relevance." The only satisfactory solution for the audience and the artist as well is to hold on to both Caliban and Ariel, the real and the imagined, actuality and potentiality. To maintain the reciprocal interaction of the two will not be easy; the temptation to grant dominance to one or the other is constant, though the problem is different for the artist than for the audience. The artist must resist his tendency to forget the ultimate intransigence of the real in the exhilaration of exercising his power over the imagined. The audience must avoid misconceiving the real and the imagined in either of two opposite ways: by merging them (treating art as magic), or by keeping them entirely disjoint (treating art as an end in itself without relevance to life).

Section three as a whole also makes explicit some of the strategic reasons behind Auden's treatment of the poem as performance. Not only does he direct the grouping and arrangement of set pieces by gauging their impact on the spectator, but he pointedly constructs the individual sections or speeches so as to make both misconceptions of the imagined world more difficult for his audience. His emphasis on the artifice and formality of art, for example, obstructs any reader who would take the poem as sufficiently real in itself. Similarly, some of his editorial practices, as we have seen, are designed to balk the impulse to seal off or categorize the poems without reading any judgment of the real world in the mirror of the imagined.

In the process of defining these improper responses to the imagined, Auden seems, incidentally, to suggest the semi-drama as a form. The semi-drama is neither realistic nor wholly abstract. In this sense it can serve to mitigate the problem of the artist in keeping his work balanced between the real and the ideal. As Caliban states the controlling paradox:

> I begin to feel something of the serio-comic embarrassment of the dedicated dramatist, who, in representing to you your condition of estrangement from the truth, is doomed to fail the more he succeeds, for the more truthfully he paints the condition, the less clearly can he indicate the truth from which it is estranged, the brighter his revelation of the truth in its order, its justice, its joy, the fainter shows his picture of your actual condition in all its drabness and sham.[28]

Auden can finally offer no sure means for resolving the artist's dilemma. At best he can hope that his art may fail in an unpredictable way, through some accident like an absurd misprint in his text. His only salvation is that at the point of recognizing his failure, the artist can see that his work has been a poor analogy for the Divine Work.[29] As a practical matter, however, the artist must still create in some particular form, and in part Auden's terms seem to propose the semi-drama. With Ariel's world, the "Heaven of the Really General Case," Auden

[28] *CP*, 399-400.

[29] The expedients which Auden must use to make this conclusion credible explain and perhaps justify the complex shifts in perspective throughout section three. The reader is asked to grasp an essential relationship between Caliban and Ariel without limiting his understanding to any particular set of terms. In relation to the human individual, Caliban is body and Ariel spirit. In aesthetic terms, Caliban is life and Ariel art. In the work's final religious perspective, Caliban stands for everything human beings are and know; Ariel becomes analogous to the "Wholly Other Life" which is "our only *raison d'être*" (*CP*, 402). Only after applying the distinction between Ariel and Caliban in a variety of perspectives can the reader be ready to make the leap of "negative knowledge" from the Caliban of earthly existence to the Ariel of Divine Otherness. See earlier discussion of "negative knowledge" in Chapter 2.

has explicitly associated allegory. An art devoted to Caliban's world, the condition of things as they are, is clearly analogous in theatrical terms to the realistic or naturalistic drama. The semi-drama, which strives to include elements of both the abstract and the realistic, is in effect Auden's development of a form that can avoid either extreme. In his poetry as a whole, however, we may note that Ariel often dominates Caliban.

Auden's third type of dramatic poem remains to be considered. By far the large majority of his short poems fall into this group of "implied dramas." In fact, most of his short poems seem able to serve as parts of semi-dramas that were never written. But without the wider context of a longer work to particularize the latent drama, these poems usually leave the reader to infer precisely what the situation involves. Character is even more shadowy than in the semi-dramas. Typically Auden presents a nameless and faceless psyche that is recording its reaction to some common human situation. Lacking a specific history or future, such figures portray states of being even more clearly than do the characters in the more formally dramatic works.[30] A fine example is "Prime" (1951), which presents a man—any man—gradually waking at dawn to resume his consciousness and his body. By the end of the poem the persona has reached a renewed awareness of his nature as a human and historical being:

> . . . this ready flesh
> No honest equal but my accomplice now,
> My assassin to be, and my name
> Stands for my historical share of care

[30] Exceptions occur in a few ballads like "Miss Gee" (1940), where Auden evidently felt that the folk-song form called for narrative character study.

For a lying self-made city,
Afraid of our living task, the dying
Which the coming day will ask.[31]

The persona, placed in this universal human situation of waking, neither has nor needs a name.

Frequently, even the dramatic situation that the protagonist faces is left largely undefined. In "The Secret Agent" (1928), not only do we know nothing of the personal history of the speaker, but Auden tells us nothing about the cause he is working for. The dramatic circumstances enter the poem only indirectly in the ominous connotations of danger associated with a spying mission. This vagueness itself allows a wide range of responses to the poem; the secret agent could easily be identified with the artist, who is another kind of confidence man. What does interest Auden is the reason for the agent's failure. Partly discouraged by an indifferent response to his recommendations, he falls into "the trap/ For a bogus guide, seduced with the old tricks." Also his alertness has been undermined by a fantasy of easy victory, "a companion/ Dreamed of already."[32] The drama is merely implied for the sake of projecting Auden's psychological study into enough of an existential situation for it to be credible.

To communicate a sense of immediacy or urgency without relying on specific character development or narration,

---

[31] First published in *Nones*. Punctuation here follows the Random House edition of *The Shield of Achilles* (p. 64). The final two lines hint at the Crucifixion and help fulfill the function of "Prime" as the first poem in the sequence of "Horae Canonicae." Such sequences of poems with a controlling theme or subject serve a purpose analogous to the semi-dramas in providing a larger context which enriches the range of meaning in each particular poem. Auden first experimented with such a grouping, though with uncertain success, in his 1928 volume.

[32] CP, 29.

Auden characteristically counts on heightened rhetoric. Many short poems employ direct address to reinforce the urgency of his point. In "The Questioner Who Sits So Sly" (1930), the speaker of the poem in effect examines a secular catechumen about his willingness to undertake the hard quest: "Will you turn a deaf ear/ To what they said on the shore,/ . . . Yet wear no ruffian badge/ . . . Carry no talisman/ . . . Never . . . make signs."[33] Also, the formal rhetorical occasion of prayer has called forth some of Auden's best short works, among them "Not, Father, further do prolong/ Our necessary defeat" (1932), and the little-known prose piece, *Litany and Anthem for St. Matthew's Day* (1946). Another device for heightening rhetoric is the use of "O" as an invocation to emphasize emotionally significant lines. Auden frequently chooses the imperative to attract attention, as in "Let the florid music praise" (1936), and "Stop all the clocks, cut off the telephone" (1940). Several such rhetorical devices may work together in a single poem. In general they have the effect of bringing the shorter poems closer to the dramatic immediacy of dialogue, for the speaking voice is usually directed not to the reader but to an audience or another character whose presence is implied by the framing of the poem.

The lack of clearly defined dramatic character and situation is paralleled by the kind of imagery which pervades these poems. Stephen Spender, without approving, has observed that in Auden's poems there is a lack of "things which are just things—trees and stars and mountains and sun."[34] Such "real" imagery would be appropriate in a

---

[33] *CP*, 177-178.
[34] "Auden and His Poetry," 77. Reprinted in *Auden*, ed. Monroe K. Spears, 34.

more traditional type of dramatic situation, where a character encounters a situation stocked with "real" obstacles. A few poems in *Homage to Clio*, written consciously to avoid self-imitation, do illustrate the type, but Auden's characteristic practice is clearly different. At most he may use purely descriptive imagery long enough to develop a tension between physical appearances and metaphysical or psychic realities. In "We All Make Mistakes" (1930), he associates physical handsomeness and psychic decay "just to make people examine the paradox."[35] Usually the paradox is resolved to give greater importance to Ariel than to the Caliban of the solidly physical. In "Dover 1937" (1940), the main interest quickly grows beyond the descriptive imagery.

> Steep roads, a tunnel through the downs are the
> approaches;
> A ruined pharos overlooks a constructed bay;
> The sea-front is almost elegant; all this show
> Has, somewhere inland, a vague and dirty root:
> Nothing is made in this town.[36]

"Somewhere inland" points to somewhere in the depths of the people and the society that make Dover. Auden will not allow the imagery to remain simply visual.

Why has Auden so consistently been drawn to dramatic structure for his poems? Why does he so often project his thoughts in dramatized metaphors of opposition, such as Caliban and Ariel, James and Michael Ransom, "We" and "They" of numerous early poems like

---

[35] "A Dialogue with W. H. Auden (with Howard Griffin)," *Partisan Review*, xx (January 1953), 81. Mr. Griffin is former private secretary to Mr. Auden. The poem cited shows a marked resemblance to E. A. Robinson's "Richard Cory." See *CP*, 51.

[36] *CP*, 111.

The Orators? The readiest explanation lies in his anti-Romanticism. Instead of personal self-expression, he presents dichotomies whose terms, by implication, ought to be involved in his reader's personal thinking. Even shadowy characters and situations help make opposites more palpable. The implied struggle or tension heightens the sense that important issues are at stake. Also, by the indirectness of dramatic projection, Auden is personally dissociated from his poems. Even when one of the characters speaks as "I," as in "Vespers" (1955), the "I" is not Auden himself, but a faceless and nameless being who happens to hold "Arcadian" views similar to his own. These are carefully balanced rhetorically and philosophically by the opposing views of the "Utopian." Instead of asserting, "This is what *I* think," Auden is implying that "The differences between these characters raise questions which must be resolved, I think, in your decisions." Auden's practice of indirection through the dramatic structuring of poems should be clear. As we shall see, his strategies on the level of verse form and technique are similarly directed at stimulating the reader, and perhaps the poet himself, to be more aware of just what his decisions involve.

CHAPTER V

VERBAL PLAYING
IN FORM AND TECHNIQUE

In critical discussion of Auden's poetry, "style" is almost unusable as a concept. He is so versatile that the styles at his command are bewilderingly diverse. He commands the formal epigrammatic force of "Art is not life and cannot be/ A mid-wife to society,"[1] as adeptly as the discursive prosiness of:

> The poet,
> Admired for his earnest habit of calling
> The sun the sun, his mind Puzzle, is made uneasy
> By these solid statues which so obviously doubt
> His antimythological myth.[2]

His diction ranges from the conventionally poetic to the technically scientific and the obscene. His manner varies appropriately with the genre in which he is working, be it song, verse epistle, or epitaph.

Ultimately, a survey of his styles would require nearly as many quotations as there are poems by Auden. Monroe Spears, by studying the poems in chronological groups and by not insisting on too rigid a scheme of classification, has succeeded in delineating a number of frequently used styles.[3] But Auden frustrates any precise taxonomy. Prominent among his reasons for trying out so many styles is

---

[1] "New Year Letter," CP, 267.

[2] "In Praise of Limestone," Nones, 15.

[3] See Poetry of Auden, especially 22-26, 145-153, 197-199, 303, 329. Inevitably, there are some problems: Can "Rilkean sonnet" (p. 25) adequately describe a style? Does the "theological light verse" (p. 197) of the 1940's mark a new style or a new subject matter for an existing style?

the desire to avoid the kind of personalism that would mark each of his works as unmistakably an "Auden poem."

> The modern poet has another tendency which he needs to watch, . . . the tendency to develop an overpersonal style and to develop it much too early in life. The temptation to do this is the same—fear of not being truly himself. I can only be certain, he seems to argue, that I am being authentically myself if everybody must admit that what I write, whether it be good or bad, at least could have been written by nobody else on earth but me. The trouble about this is that a person can and ought to change; at any given time his being holds latent possibilities which are waiting their chance to realize themselves. An overpersonal style, no matter how authentic so far as it goes, becomes a prison from which the poet cannot escape.[4]

Auden's terms here suggest another reason for his many styles and for his wide ranging among poetic forms. The process of playing within the confines of a particular style or verse form can aid the poet in realizing the possibilities latent in the self and the imagination. Usually we assume that a new insight stimulates a poet to develop a new style; Auden, on the other hand, seeks out new styles as a means to discovering new insights.

As many critics have suggested, then, Auden is a stylistic chameleon, but a less direct means of talking about his poetic manner may be more fruitful. I want to appropriate temporarily the word "technique" to refer to a habitual way he has of joining words and phrases, one which appears in a broad range of poems. I submit that after 1935 there gradually emerges in Auden's poetry

[4] "The Dyer's Hand," 292.

an inclination to use words and images in an "unserious" way, regardless of how we might categorize the style of any individual poem. However serious their subject or theme, Auden's mature poems most often have the flavor of comic verse in which the droll image or the witty incongruity may appear at any moment. "Dame Kind" (1960) displays the unserious technique in pure form:

> Steatopygous, sow-dugged
>
> and owl-headed,
> To Whom—Whom else?—the first innocent blood
>
> was formally shed
> By a chinned mammal that hard times
>
> had turned carnivore,
> From Whom his first promiscuous orgy
>
> begged a downpour
> To speed the body-building cereals
>
> of a warmer age:
> Now who put *us*, we should like to know,
>
> in *Her* manage?[5]

This poem is richly comic in the apparent arbitrariness of its word choices and its choppy, conversational flow. The subject—man's unfortunate subjection to the natural drives within him—is serious; the technique, obviously, is not.

In 1964 Auden clarifies some of the thinking that leads him to such distinctive speech rhythms and the striking mixture of homely and *outré* diction. He says: "I want every poem I write to be a hymn in praise of the English

[5] *Homage to Clio*, 53. Howard Griffin reminds us that Auden owns the 12-volume unabridged Oxford English Dictionary; many of his poems in the last twenty years are likely to send the reader to the same word-hoard. See "A Dialogue with W. H. Auden," *Hudson Review*, III (Winter 1951), 575.

language: hence my fascination with certain speech-rhythms which can only occur in an uninflected language rich in monosyllables, my fondness for peculiar words with no equivalents in other tongues, and my deliberate avoidance of that kind of visual imagery which has no basis in verbal experience and can therefore be translated without loss."[6]

Such homage to the untranslatable in the English language is unmistakable in "Dame Kind." Italics and punctuation insist that the lines be read with a single conversational inflection that not only cues important meanings, but brings the speaking voice dramatically to life. Homage is implicit also in the arresting diction. Auden chooses unexpected words like "steatopygous," "carnivore," and "sow-dugged," which recapitulate the unique composition of English out of Greek, Latin, and Anglo-Saxon roots. To work as closely as Auden does with a hodgepodge like colloquial English leads almost inevitably to an unserious poetic treatment of whatever subject.

As a beginning poet, Auden was not instinctively drawn to an unserious technique. His early work suggests that he took himself as a more serious or vatic poet. Starting about 1935, however, he began the experiments in light verse which proved to be the testing ground for his mature technique. By 1940 he had written many of his songs, had tried out music-hall satire in his plays, and had worked substantially in the popular vein. We might fruitfully digress to consider the seeds of his mature technique as they grew during his most concentrated cultivation of the field of light verse. Conveniently, Auden has provided working definitions in his 1938 anthology, *The*

[6] "Symposium," *Kenyon Review*, xxvi (Winter 1964), 207-208. Reprinted in *The Contemporary Poet*, ed. Anthony Ostroff, 186.

Oxford Book of Light Verse, itself evidence for his interest in and wide knowledge of such poetry. Three kinds of poetry, he says, are included in this volume:

(1) Poetry written for performance, to be spoken or sung before an audience [e.g. Folk-songs, the poems of Tom Moore].

(2) Poetry intended to be read, but having for its subject-matter the everyday social life of its period or the experiences of the poet as an ordinary human being [e.g. the poems of Chaucer, Pope, Byron].

(3) Such nonsense poetry as, through its properties and technique, has a general appeal [e.g. nursery rhymes, the poems of Edward Lear].[7]

In all but the last category, Auden's own practice has been considerable. He devotes an entire forty-two-page section of his *Collected Poetry* to "Songs and Other Musical Pieces." Into his second category fall many of his shorter poems and, most obviously, "Letter to Lord Byron" (1937). Finally, although Auden has written little nonsense poetry, he does offer a personal tribute to the poets in his third category.

> You must ask me who
> Have written just as I'd have liked to do.
> I stop to listen and the names I hear
> Are those of Firbank, Potter, Carroll, Lear.[8]

Also in his criticism he consistently praises poets who, like Byron, succeed as long as they take nothing very seriously.[9]

The appeal of light verse for Auden goes beyond personal pleasure. In the perspective of cultural history he

[7] "Introduction" to *The Oxford Book of Light Verse* (London, 1938), ix.
[8] "Letter to Lord Byron," *Letters from Iceland*, 202.
[9] *The Oxford Book of Light Verse*, xvii.

finds that lightness in poetry reflects an intimate relation between the poet and his audience. The modern poet who inherits no sense of community with his readers finds himself in a paradoxical situation. His estrangement from society allows him to see its faults; yet that same isolation makes communication of his insights proportionately more difficult.[10] What Auden *can* do, recognizing the problem, is to manufacture lightness as a possible means of reopening communication. In the late 1930's light verse seemed to Auden for a time a promising means for reaching a large audience. It also served indirectly as a stimulus to developing his unserious technique. It suggested striking variations on old saws or folk figures presumably having wide cultural dissemination. It sanctioned verse forms in which colloquial diction and witty rimes were appropriate. It provided a vehicle for treating serious subjects in an ironically lowbrow manner.

Auden never succeeded in reaching as wide an audience as he had hoped. Even in 1936, in the midst of his most direct efforts at public appeal, he remarked, "Personally, the kind of poetry I should like to write but can't is 'the thoughts of a wise man in the speech of the common people.' "[11] The subjects he wanted to treat in verse became, especially after 1940, less amenable to presentation in a popular mode, and he resigned himself to the fact that for poetry that is not propaganda, the audience is inescapably limited. He continued to extol the virtues of lowbrow art, but less in hopes of a real *rapprochement* than with the intent of unsettling highbrow prejudices.[12]

[10] *Ibid.*, x-xi.
[11] "Poets, Poetry, and Taste," *The Highway*, xxxix (December 1936), 44.
[12] See, for example, his "Address on Henry James," *Gazette of the Grolier Club*, ii (February 1947), 211-225.

More recently he labels himself a highbrow while mourning the extinction of popular art in the postwar culture built by mass media.[13]

From his attempts at popular light verse, however, Auden did preserve an inclination toward unserious poetic technique. A close look at one representative poem may reveal the genesis of the technique that appears in some measure in nearly all of his poems in the last twenty-five years. Auden tried out every conceivable light verse form, from the madrigal and the "blues" to the limerick and clerihew, but one of his most exemplary productions is the ballad, "As I walked out one evening" (1940).[14] The poem is introduced by a common folk-song mouthpiece, the passive observer whose reports appear trustworthy because they are carefully detailed: he even specifies that his walk took him down Bristol Street. This persona disappears in the second stanza behind the lover, who is overheard singing from under an arch of the railway. The location of the lovers, implying a quick mating under the bridge, is an early sign for the forthcoming deflation of the singer's Romantic exaggerations. His song is filled with overstated claims for his love in typical folk-song manner:[15]

> I'll love you till the ocean
> Is folded and hung up to dry,

[13] See "The Dyer's Hand," 296, and DH, 83.

[14] CP, 197-199. The urge to comment on this fine poem is irresistible, despite the inevitability of repeating some points made or implied in such valuable analyses as appear in Spears, Poetry of Auden, 110-112, and Cleanth Brooks and Robert Penn Warren, Understanding Poetry, 3rd ed. (New York, 1960), 332-335. See also Edward C. McAleer, "As Auden Walked Out," College English, XVIII (February 1957), 271-272.

[15] That Auden still finds such poetic inflations useful to play against is evident in "Dichtung und Wahrheit," Homage to Clio, 48. Italics in the following two quotations are mine.

> And the seven stars go squawking
>> Like geese about the sky.

> The years shall run like rabbits,
>> For in my arms I *hold*
> The flower of the Ages,
>> And the first love of the *world*.

The off-rime here in the fifth stanza, one of the two in the poem, undercuts the fantasy. Time begins its counter-insistence in stanza six. In stanza seven the second off-rime, coupled this time with a pointed alliteration, rein-forces the disrupting power of Time:

> In the burrows of the Nightmare
>> Where Justice naked *is*,
> Time watches from the shadow
>> And *c*oughs when you would *k*iss.

In stanzas six through fourteen, Time insistently cata-logues the terrors of human existence. One incisive de-scription of this "land of the dead" depicts an inversion of the pleasant fairytale world of childhood:

> Where the beggars raffle the banknotes
>> And the Giant is enchanting to Jack,
> And the Lily-white Boy is a Roarer,
>> And Jill goes down on her back.

The unexpected colloquialism in the last line, further emphasized by rime, is most effective. The reader is startled into greater attention by the slang that he may never have encountered before in a poem. At the same time the crude associations of "on her back" convey precisely what has happened to the innocent nursery-rime world of Jack and Jill. The poem concludes with the only resolution possible: the brimming river, linked in stanza two with the lover's overflowing emotions, now rushes on, imperturbable and inhuman.

> It was late, late in the evening,
> The lovers they were gone;
> The clocks had ceased their chiming,
> And the deep river ran on.

While maintaining a level of exaggeration in imagery which is consonant with the folk-song framework, the poem has refused to accept as binding either sentimental love or the norms of polite poetic diction. It is vigorously direct in making its point; yet it retains the ease and flexibility of a folk ballad. Within some limits, the lover's song could have been longer or shorter; so could Time's counter-song. One or two stanzas added or deleted would not crucially modify the poem.[16] While this accordion-like expandability is entirely appropriate to the ballad form, the apparent looseness of the poem is somewhat deceptive. Even the putative folk-poet faces imaginative restrictions. If a ballad is to be singable, as Auden apparently intended most of his to be,[17] each stanza must

[16] The majority of revisions Auden made for his *CP* as studied by Joseph Warren Beach in his *Auden Canon* take the form of the deletion of stanzas. One might conclude that the stanza is the basic building block of most of Auden's poems and that many more of his poems than the popular ballads share their characteristic expandable structure.

[17] Auden designated tunes for two of the ballads reprinted in *CP*: "Miss Gee," 209-213, to "The St. James Infirmary," and "Victor," 233-238, to "Frankie and Johnny." This writer has tried singing "As I walked out one evening" to the tune of "The Logger Lover," which begins, in one version:

> As I sat down one evening,
> 'Twas in a small cafe,

conform to the same basic pattern of accents in order to fit a single tune. This ballad is highly effective when read aloud, but also, granted standard folk-song license to cram several syllables into a short musical space, it meets the demands of singability. In several perspectives, then, this poem with its publicly available imagery set in an appropriate form is a successful attempt at modern light verse.

The single most important facet of technique that Auden explored primarily in such light verse and then carried over into more serious works involves what we might call the principle of poetic unexpectedness. Like all the memorable comic and satiric poets, he seems to have understood instinctively what his reading of Kierkegaard reinforced: the most direct source of aesthetic interest is the unexpected or incongruous. Thus a clergyman who steals is aesthetically interesting; one who simply performs all his duties properly is dull.[18] To exploit this principle, Auden establishes in the reader's mind a series of expectations which he then disappoints by injecting the incongruous. The expectations can either be generated within the poem itself or be assumed to exist in the reader's mind. "As I walked out" works in both ways. Early in the poem the lover expresses an extravagant Romantic infatuation, which no one is expected to take seriously. For the reader, however, these images tempo-

---

A forty-year-old waitress
To me these words did say.

For the tune and further words see *The New Songfest*, ed. Dick and Beth Best (New York, 1955), 36. The first lines of Auden's poem and this song, although interestingly similar, are too much common folk property to allow the suggestion of particular influence.

[18] See "A Preface to Kierkegaard," *The New Republic*, cx (May 15, 1944), 683-686.

rarily constitute the basic terms of this particular poem. By the time he has read to stanza five, where the song ends, the reader presumably anticipates that the poem will continue with more of the same sentimental overstatement. There are, it is true, ominous anticipations of the coming destruction of the Romanticized ideal, like the off-rime on "world" that we have discussed and the implications of the image in the first stanza: "The crowds upon the pavement/ Were fields of harvest wheat." But these hints are not brought home until the sixth stanza, when Time and his scythe enter dramatically to reverse the reader's expectations.

This same poem also upsets associations that the reader will likely bring to the poem. The single line, "And Jill goes down on her back," presumes for its impact that the reader has idealized Edenic associations with the childhood world of nursery rime and that he holds a rather conventional notion of proper poetic diction. The unexpected fate of Jill is aimed at shocking any unthinking nostalgia a reader may have. The effectiveness of this device, we may note, depends on its ability to surprise and reorient the associations of the reader. If he does not bring the expected associations with him to the poem or cannot imaginatively assume them, the device may fall flat.

The number of images and associations that modern readers can be expected to have in common is extremely limited. Hence, when he aims more directly at a highbrow audience, Auden must count on the knowledge a sophisticated reader carries with him. In "New Year Letter," for instance, in order to present a similarly anti-Romantic view of the present world he calls on less common knowledge: "But wishes are not horses, this/ *Annus* is not

mirabilis."[19] Nearly all readers follow the poem's variation on the old maxim about beggars and horses, but
only the educated can recognize the playful parody of
Dryden's title.

In its most sophisticated and highbrow form, the allusion with an unexpected variation can reach only a
highly specialized audience. The first stanza of "Song
for St. Cecilia's Day" (1945), for example, reads as
follows:

> In a garden shady this holy lady
> With reverent cadence and subtle psalm,
> Like a black swan as death came on
> Poured forth her song in perfect calm:[20]

Only a reader versed in madrigals would recognize that
here Auden is transforming part of the anonymous lyric
to Orlando Gibbons' piece, "The Silver Swan."

> The silver swan who, living, had no note,
> When death approached, unlocked her silent throat:
> Leaning her breast against the reedy shore,
> Thus sang her first and last, and sang no more.[21]

Specialized though it is, the allusion to a madrigal is
certainly appropriate in a poem for St. Cecilia, the patron
saint of music. The twisting of the original context, the
transmutation of the silver swan into black garb, calls
particular attention to St. Cecilia's nunlike qualities, which
in turn reflect the poem's view of her music as an earthly
analogue to a heavenly order.

Auden can also play against expectations and associa-

19 CP, 313.
20 CP, 203.
21 *The A Cappella Singer*, ed. H. Clough-Leighter (Boston, 1936),
68-71.

tions conventionally attached to the dramatic circumstances of a poem. "Many Happy Returns" (1945) is a birthday letter to a seven-year-old boy, but its good wishes express nothing of the conventional hopes for material advantage or happiness that the situation would lead one to anticipate. Relaxed and disarmed by the direct address to the boy, the informality of contractions, and the carefully simple diction, a reader may be startled by the sophisticated and adult advice the poem offers:

> So I wish you first a
> Sense of theatre; only
> Those who love illusion
> And know it will go far:
> Otherwise we spend our
> Lives in a confusion
> Of what we say and do with
> Who we really are.
>
> . . . .
>
> Just because our pride's an
> Evil there's no end to,
> Birthdays and the arts are
> Justified, for when
> We consciously pretend to
> Own the earth or play at
> Being gods, thereby we
> Own that we are men.[22]

The short lines play a particularly important part in giving the superficial impression of simplicity, but the familiar Auden richness is there, as in the double meaning of "Those who love illusion/ And know it." Also a

[22] CP, 68-69. Monroe Spears suggests the important function of situation in this poem. See Poetry of Auden, 197.

double feminine rime links the two halves of nearly all stanzas.

Auden can put the general idea of poetic unpredictability to other and more startling uses. He may even challenge a reader's grasp on the logic by which language is made into statements. Four lines from "Air Port" (1951) can illustrate:

> Let out where two fears intersect, a point selected
> Jointly by general staffs and engineers,
> In a wet land, facing rough oceans, never invaded
> By Caesars or a cartesian doubt, I stand. . . .[23]

The initial description of physical landscape in emotional terms is familiar enough to Auden's readers, and if the two fears have controlled the decisions of two unexpected groups, at least soldiers and scientists are all human beings. But the leap of mind which makes Caesars and cartesian doubts parallel is enough to make a reader, but for the title, puzzle over just what the context is. On reflection one can see that the general staffs are absurd in a land that has never been of interest to Caesars, and engineers seem out of place where people are not self-conscious enough to conceive cartesian doubts, let alone develop a technology philosophically based on them. The apparently random juxtaposition of contexts and images has served its purpose, however, by eliciting a serious effort at comprehension by means of elegant incongruity.

One further example of Auden's use of the unexpected involves the posing of apparent paradox. The context is a fairly serious section of "Music is International" (1951):

> To forgive is not so
> Simple as it is made to sound; a lot

[23] *Nones*, 23.

Of time will be quite wasted, many
Promising days end badly and again
We shall offend: but let us listen
To the song which seems to absorb all this,
For these halcyon structures are useful
As structures go—though not to be confused
With anything really important
Like feeding strays or looking pleased when caught
By a bore or a hideola;[24]

The unexpected particularization provided by the concluding similes is purposely incongruous at first contact. There is nothing ostensibly "important" about feeding strays or restraining one's reaction to a bore. On second thought, however, the reader can see these apparently trivial events in a serious religious perspective. Auden insists that forgiving or loving one's neighbor is the only serious business of life and this religious principle must be applied to the most unlikely situations and unlovable people or it has not been effectively lived. The apparent paradox in the meaning of "important" has not only arrested the reader's attention, but has reinforced the vital metaphysical point.

The diverse application of poetic unexpectedness or incongruity seems at the heart of Auden's mature technique and his inclination toward making serious points in an unserious way. Among other things this technique reinforces his characteristic kind of ambiguity. Unlike the unresolvable obscurity of some of his early poems, this is the temporary ambiguity of a riddle. Once the reader has exerted the conscious effort required to solve it, he can see the riddle as a rhetorically arresting and elegant

[24] *Nones*, 73. This was the Phi Beta Kappa poem at Columbia University in 1947.

combination of words that also contains an unforeseen yet inescapable comment on human nature or a human problem. Because the poem's comment is made by upsetting and reordering his previous associations with the words or situations involved, the reader may be startled into accepting a fresh evaluation of himself and his world. Ideally, he will go on to take the verbal meaning "seriously" by attempting to rethink his life on the basis of the poem's insights. What poetic technique can do is to lead him to understand the verbal formulas against which he can measure conduct. Unfortunately, as Auden has several times remarked with some annoyance, the educated in particular find it easy to be satisfied with a purely intellectual understanding; one of the great dangers of language, as he says, is that "it can always think of reasons."[25]

At any point the reader may choose simply to savor the aesthetic pleasure provided by the neatness and elegance of a riddle's verbal structure, or he may be satisfied to accept the implied compliment if he recognizes the source of an allusion. Such responses would seem particularly appropriate to some of Auden's recent poems, since they function primarily as vehicles for verbal playing. Auden clearly delights in exercising his skill at composing a witty and elegant statement on whatever subject he chooses. One of the thirty-four clerihews from *Homage to Clio* can illustrate the kind of *vers de société* that sometimes results:

> When the young Kant
> Was told to kiss his aunt,
> He obeyed the Categorical Must,
> But only just.[26]

[25] "A Dialogue with W. H. Auden," *Hudson Review*, III (Winter 1951), 579. See also, "Squares and Oblongs," 180.
[26] "Academic Graffiti," *Homage to Clio*, 87.

The neatness of this little poem lies in its placing of Kant's somber philosophical principle in a relatively trivial though genuinely human setting of boyish embarrassment. The unexpected shortness of the last line reinforces the humorous incongruity of the abstract doctrine applied in the living situation. Beyond this genially irreverent mocking of pompous intellectualism, the poem can hardly be said to have a serious point. The poet seems to invite the reader to share in the sophisticated fun of seeing what words can do.

The grounds of Auden's mature interest in an unserious poetic technique become clear in his rationale for such conscious trifling in poetry. In defense of fun he prefers a "European" conception of poetry to American overseriousness.

> American poetry has many tones. . . , but the easy-going tone of a man talking to a group of his peers is rare; for a "serious" poet to write light verse is frowned on in America and if, when he is asked why he writes poetry, he replies, as any European poet would, "For fun," his audience will be shocked. (In this Cambridge-on-the-Cam is perhaps a few leagues nearer Gambier, Ohio than is Oxford-on-Thames.)[27]

Part of Auden's ultimate rationale goes beyond the implications of this relatively light-hearted statement to a more serious insistence on the value of play in the face of a depersonalized modern world.

> Why should the authorities feel that a highbrow artist is important enough to be worth destroying? It can only

[27] "The Anglo-American Difference," *The Anchor Review*, No. 1 (1955), 216. *DH*, 366, deletes the parenthetical slap at the younger years of *Kenyon Review* and *Scrutiny*.

be because so long as artists exist, making what they please even if it is not very good, even if few people appreciate it, they remind the management of something the management does not like to be reminded of, namely, that the managed people are people with faces, not anonymous numbers; it reminds them that *Homo sapiens* is also *Homo ludens* which, if admitted, makes nonsense of any doctrine of historical necessity.[28]

Stephen Spender has suggested that a kind of frivolity is dominant in Auden's mode of poetry. He calls it a "serious insistence on unseriousness—on reducing the cosmos to the personal and gossipy even."[29] Certainly Auden's handling of intensely serious subjects in apparently trivial terms is one of his most pervasive and delightful uses of poetic incongruity. His aim, however, is not often simply reductive. Auden's position as he has extended it in the last fifteen years comes close to being a serious insistence on the impossibility of being serious in poetry.

This rather paradoxical position grows by stages out of Auden's mature conception of man. We have seen that by 1940 or so he was convinced that direct sincerity is a pretense which can only lead to self-deception and falsehood. As "New Year Letter" indicates, an unserious technique seemed to Auden at that time an aid to trapping the elusive truth and making it available to the conscious mind:

> Though Language may be useless, for
> No words men write can stop the war

[28] "The Dyer's Hand," 300. *DH*, 88, adapts this passage deleting the reference to highbrow art and the implied rejection of Marxism.
[29] "Seriously Unserious," *Poetry* [Chicago] LXXVIII (September 1951), 352.

Or measure up to the relief
Of its immeasurable grief,
Yet truth, like love and sleep, resents
Approaches that are too intense,
And often when the searcher stood
Before the Oracle, it would
Ignore his grown-up earnestness
But not the child of his distress,
For through the Janus of a joke
The candid psychopompos spoke.[30]

The psychopompos, Hermes, the guide of the souls of the dead, may be induced to speak through a joke which can look two ways; if on one side it is not intended to be honest self-expression, it has the chance of being truthful on the other. The truth that the poem as joke reveals, of course, may turn out to be that the human being cannot speak truth. Even then the poem, which is itself an instance of human play-acting, can reveal to men something of themselves as actors who may never be able to catch themselves off-stage to see what they are "really" like.

This line of thinking is developed more fully in "The Truest Poetry is the Most Feigning" (1955), originally subtitled "Ars Poetica for Hard Times."[31] It concludes:

For, given Man, by birth, by education,
Imago Dei who forgot his station,
The self-made creature who himself unmakes,
The only creature ever made who fakes,
With no more nature in his loving smile
Than in his theories of a natural style,

[30] CP, 273-274.
[31] New Yorker, xxx (November 13, 1954), 44.

What but tall tales, the luck of verbal playing,
Can trick his lying nature into saying
That love, or truth in any serious sense,
Like orthodoxy, is a reticence.[32]

Reiterating Auden's conception of man as actor, this poem implies that the poet can say something true only by accident, by the "luck of verbal playing" with an unserious technique within the limitations of verse form. The final "truth" that emerges, however, is paradoxical: the poem asserts that truth in any serious sense is a reticence, something that is unspeakable in poetry or in prose. In the words of an earlier couplet from the same poem, "No metaphor, remember, can express/ A real historical unhappiness." The most feigning poetry is the truest because its artifice gives public recognition to its inability to state directly a truth that has any necessary validity outside the poem; hence, it is truest to the limitations of poetry.

Auden's most recent attack on this problem, appropriately entitled "Dichtung und Wahrheit" (1960), is not actually a poem at all, but a series of fifty short prose paragraphs pondering the difficulty of writing a poem that says "I love you" in a way that is "true." Auden concludes: "This poem I wished to write was to have expressed exactly what I mean when I think the words *I love you*, but I cannot know exactly what I mean; it was to have been self-evidently true, but words cannot verify themselves. So this poem will remain unwritten."[33] "Dichtung und Wahrheit" is not only, in the words of its subtitle, "An Unwritten Poem" but also it is unwritable as a poem. This

[32] *The Shield of Achilles,* 46.
[33] *Homage to Clio,* 48.

conclusion has not announced Auden's retirement from poetry, but it does suggest that in the future he may concentrate more on poems which, like his clerihew on Kant, avoid even an unserious attempt at seriousness. On the other hand, such predictions are hazardous since Auden shows little sign of diminishing creativity. He has earned the accomplished artist's right to make condescending and flip remarks about his craft, and most of his apparently self-defeating statements themselves occur in the playful medium of poetry.

What Auden has insisted on since 1940 is that the world of poetry must be taken as no more serious in itself than "playful hypothesis."[34] We have seen already how his editorial practices and his characteristic construction of long poems help remind the reader of the artificiality of art. On the level of technique a number of the devices described earlier serve this same purpose among others. The linking of words from incongruous contexts and the posing of apparent paradoxes, for example, interrupt the flow of the reader's comprehension and thus make him conscious of the verbal manipulation of meaning. A parallel technique might be called the self-deflating exaggeration. In the lover's song in "As I walked out," the assertion that this is the first love of the world is too incredibly naïve to be taken seriously by anyone likely to be reading such poetry. The reader is immediately made aware that he is in a world of "poetic" exaggeration. Most notably in *The Orators*, Auden sometimes uses a surrealistic dream imagery which must necessarily be accepted as fantastic. On occasion he may intervene directly in a poem to undercut the seriousness of poetic assertions. In "Law Like Love" (1940), he begins by rehearsing the

[34] "The Dyer's Hand," 299.

parochial definitions assigned to "the Law" by different groups of people; then, before making his own suggestion that it is like love, he interrupts with an aside:

> If therefore thinking it absurd
> To identify Law with some other word,
> Unlike so many men
> I cannot say Law is again,
>
> . . . .
>
> Although I can at least confine
> Your vanity and mine
> To stating timidly
> A timid similarity,
> We shall boast anyway:
> Like love I say.[35]

Not only do these remarks interrupt the poem's catalog of the possible meanings of Law, but also they attack all verbal identities or definitions as absurd. Auden himself will pointedly offer only similes, the least assertive form of comparison. In fact, Auden's concluding simile is so guarded and qualified by his rebuff of the earlier "definitions" of Law that the reader is likely to be surprised when the "timid similarity" turns out to have considerable aptness and force:

> Like love we don't know where or why
> Like love we can't compel or fly
> Like love we often weep
> Like love we seldom keep.

In his opera libretti especially, we can see Auden cultivating a genre for the sake of its artifice. The incredible

[35] CP, 76.

exaggeration in operatic plot, character, and spectacle—
in fact, the grand manner itself—is the genius of the
medium to Auden: "For a singer, as for a ballet dancer,
there is no question of simulation, of singing a composer's
notes 'naturally'; his behavior is unabashedly and tri-
umphantly art from beginning to end."[36] Auden's understanding of the role of art differs sharply from that of
someone like Henry James, who is equally aware that art
is artifice. James wants to carry off the effect, to lull the
reader into forgetting that the artifact is "a verbal contraption."[37] Auden wants precisely the opposite, and he is
willing to go to considerable lengths to use the contrivance
of the verbal world to throw the reader back on himself.

For the poet as moralist, the value of playing the game
of poetry resides in its potential ability to circumvent or
at least lay bare the self-deception inherent in the conscious mental processes of human beings. Auden, by
parading the fact that the poem is a performance by
one actor—the poet—may trap the reader into recognizing
that he also is an actor. For the poet himself, moreover,
unserious verbal playing with technique and verse form
may help to outwit his own defensive rationalizations.
Fulfilling the formal requirements of a poem can assist
him toward that impersonality whereby the conscious
mind of the poet does not speak, but the *poem* does.

It is dangerous for criticism to go behind the closed
doors of the poet's workroom to comment on his process
of creation, but Auden's own revelations, particularly on
the role of poetic form, seem worthy of attention. While

[36] "Some Reflections on Opera as a Medium," *Tempo* [London],
No. 20 (Summer 1951), 7. DH, 468.
[37] *Making, Knowing, and Judging*, 23. DH, 50.

he is certainly aware of the impossibility of maintaining a perfectly clear distinction between form and content, he feels free to make some leading remarks about verse forms:

> The choice of a verse form is only half conscious. No form will express everything, as each form is particularly good at expressing something. Forms are chosen by poets because the most important part of what they have to say seems to go better with that form than any other. . . , and then, in its turn, the form develops and shapes the poet's imagination so that he says things which he did not know he was capable of saying, and at the same time those parts of his imagination which once had other things to say, dry up from lack of use.[38]

Apparently, once Auden has committed a poem to a form he deems satisfactory, he relies on the dictates of that form to direct and shape what is said within it. In 1948 he puts it in the form of a neat commonplace: "How can I know what I think till I see what I say?"[39]

---

[38] "Pope," in *From Anne to Victoria*, ed. Bonamy Dobrée (New York, 1937), 100. Reprinted in *Essays in Criticism*, 1 (July 1951), 217-218. See also "Don Juan," *DH*, 386-406, for an example of Auden's sensitivity to the contribution of form to the work of another poet.

[39] "Squares and Oblongs," 174; adapted in *DH*, 22. Auden reiterates this basic proposition as part of a balanced reconsideration of the role of craftsmanship in the act of creation; see *DH*, 67. The working manuscript for "The Sea and the Mirror," which is in the Lockwood Memorial Library at the University of Buffalo, supports these general conclusions. In the case of Miranda's villanelle, once he was sure of the form, he sketched the requirements of repetition in the margin ahead of his writing in order to test alternative phrases. See brief comments in Phyllis Bartlett, *Poems in Process* (New York, 1951), 97, and fuller description in Spears, *Poetry of Auden*, 247, n. 41, and 249, n. 48.

Verse form seems especially important in Auden's process of creation. To support his own statements we have his far-ranging exploration of different forms, which reflects more than simply a craftsman's interest in the tools of his trade. Auden has wanted to try out what he could do in virtually every form that is possible in an uninflected language like modern English, and even some that are not quite possible, like the skaldic Drott-Kvaett.[40] Perhaps his most dazzling piece of virtuosity is in "Canzone" (1945), where sixty-five lines employ only five rime words altogether.[41] Besides all the more common traditional forms he has succeeded at working within other fixed forms particularly demanding for modern English: the ballade,[42] the rondeau,[43] the villanelle,[44] the sestina,[45] and perhaps even the pantoum.[46] The only form which

[40] See *The Age of Anxiety*, 111. The form is described in E[ric] V. Gordon, *Introduction to Old Norse Verse* (Oxford, 1927), 295-297.

[41] *CP*, 161-163. This form in Auden's hands has five stanzas of twelve lines and an envoy of five lines. Each line of the envoy ends in one of the five rime words in the order (aedcb) established by taking in sequence the first rime word in each of the five basic stanzas. The same order of rime words is maintained in all second lines, third lines, and so on. The intricate rime patterns set up and maintained throughout the poem can best be appreciated in a diagram.

```
Stanza                                            Envoy
  I      a b aa c aa dd a ee                        a
  II     e a ee b ee cc e dd                        e
  III    d e dd a dd bb d cc                        d
  IV     c d cc e cc aa c bb                         c
  V      b c bb d bb ee b aa                        b
```

[42] Stephano's speech in "The Sea and the Mirror," *CP*, 362-363.

[43] "Area sub Lege" (1941), *CP*, 117-118.

[44] "Are You There?" (1945), *CP*, 35, and Miranda's speech in "The Sea and the Mirror," *CP*, 372-373.

[45] See, among others, the four sestinas comprising "Kairos and Logos," *CP*, 11-16.

[46] This form was adapted from a Malay chant by Victor Hugo. It

Auden is conscious of having attempted without publishable success is the triolet.[47]

The appeal of such traditional forms for Auden lies less in their belonging to the poetic heritage than in the complex and impersonal demands they make on his creative faculties. In the last twenty years he has created for himself a number of unique forms which are as demanding as those he borrowed from earlier poets. In some of these poems, particularly since his alliterative experiments in *The Age of Anxiety*,[48] Auden conceals formal intricacy behind a complex scheme of internal rime. "Streams" (1955) maintains the same interlocking pattern through eighteen stanzas. Three stanzas can serve as illustration:

How could we love the absent one if you did not keep
Coming from a distance, or quite directly assist,
    As when past Iseult's tower you floated
  The willow pash-notes of wanted Tristram?

And *Homo Ludens*, surely, is your child, who make
Fun of our feuds by opposing identical banks,
    Transferring the loam from Huppim
  To Muppim and back each time you crankle.

contains an indefinite number of quatrains, which are related by making the second and fourth lines of each stanza identical with the first and third lines of the next quatrain. In the final stanza the second and fourth lines are identical with the third and first lines, respectively, of the first stanza. "Nursery Rhyme," *Nones*, 35, appears to be an adaptation of this form based on repeated images rather than repeated lines. With its added refrain, the form also bears some resemblance to the medieval Spanish *cossante* discussed by Monroe Spears in *Poetry of Auden*, 320-321.

[47] Mr. Auden remarked on this failure in an interview with this writer, March 1961.

[48] For a stimulating assessment, perhaps unduly stringent, see Christine Brooke-Rose, "Notes on the Metre of Auden's *The Age of Anxiety*," *Essays in Criticism*, XIII (July 1963), 253-264.

Growth cannot add to your song: as unchristened brooks
Already you whisper to ants what, as Brahma's son,
    Descending his titanic staircase
Into Assam, to Himalayan bears you thunder.[49]

The apparently arbitrary imagery and whimsical diction
are in part necessitated by the demands of rime and line
length, but they serve at the same time to conceal the
severity of the demands made on the poet's control over
language. At first encounter the poem appears to be an
informal urbane discourse with occasional, almost chance
riming and witty puns, like the overtones of "loan" in
the "loam" from the "banks" in the second stanza quoted.
Only on close examination does the ingenuity the poet
demands from himself become evident.

Unique creations like "Streams" and traditional stanzaic
forms predominate in Auden's mature verse. He is much
attracted to an easy conversational tone and flexible
rhythm which, in the fixed forms, constitute a *tour de
force* that cannot be repeated indefinitely. Less obviously
complex forms allow him to disguise formal control behind apparent ease and fluidity. By 1940 he had followed
Marianne Moore into syllable-counting verse.[50] His early

[49] *The Shield of Achilles*, 28-31. In each quatrain the first two
lines have twelve syllables and a masculine ending; lines three and
four have feminine endings and nine and eleven syllables respectively.
The final syllable of line two rimes with the penultimate syllable of
line four; the penultimate syllable of line three rimes with another
syllable in line four. Also one syllable in line one rimes with another syllable in line three. Adapted from Auden's notes to Caedmon
recording TC 1019, *W. H. Auden Reading His Poems*.

[50] See Auden's tributes to Miss Moore in "New Poems," *New
York Times Book Review* (October 1, 1944), 7, and *DH*, 296-305.
"Spring 1940" and "Autumn 1940" (1941) both follow the same
syllabic pattern. They are composed of eleven and eighteen quatrains

poetry, written while he still felt that poems should not be written in traditional forms,[51] frequently relies on the somewhat looser control of counting stresses in each line.

After the relatively free early poems, Auden's mature verse, starting in the middle 1930's, embodies a deep commitment to precision of formal control as a means to controlling and stimulating his imagination. On the one hand, the impersonal rules of a given form will allow his imagination to express only what that form can say, not whatever he happens to have on his mind. On the other hand, the process of meeting rigid formal demands may help him articulate thoughts he could not otherwise have conceived. Every poetic form, then, may lead Auden to discover new insights in the process of expressing them.

A recognition of this contribution of form to Auden's poems is a valuable corrective to the tendency to overstate the extent to which he is a conscious artist. While most of his themes insist on consciousness, choice, and will, the making of his poems depends only in part on conscious artistic craftsmanship. A verse form interposed between his consciously thought-out control and a poem is one means he can use to avoid repeating old conclusions in familiar words. One further comment by Auden may reinforce this description of creation as discovery:

Those who confine themselves to free verse because they

---

respectively, with eleven, eleven, nine, and ten syllables in the lines of each stanza. In locating Auden's initial use of syllabic verse thus early, I differ with both G. S. Fraser and Monroe Spears. See *Poetry of Auden*, 248, n. 43.

[51] So reports Stephen Spender in "W. H. Auden and His Poetry," 74. Reprinted in *Auden*, ed. Monroe K. Spears, 27. On the formal models for Auden's early verse see Spears, *Poetry of Auden*, 21-23.

imagine that strict forms must of necessity lead to dis-
honesty, do not understand the nature of art, how little
the conscious artist can do and what large and mysterious beauties are the gifts of language, tradition and
pure accident.[52]

Taking at face value Auden's description of the impact
of strict forms on his work, we can suggest that the form
allows him to tap the reservoirs of potential poetic material which lie below consciousness. Hence, an important
reason for Auden's wide ranging among and beyond existing forms seems to be a continuing search for new areas
in himself that can be brought into the open without de-
pending on conscious intellectualizing. When it is the
poem that expresses thoughts, Auden, at least in part,
becomes a spectator to the performance of his own imagination.

In the final stage of composition, after his imagination
has met the formal demands on it with fresh poetic statements, Auden can deploy the resulting poem to suit the
occasion and the audience which he has projected for
himself. He may change the context in which he wants
it to be read, as with the Vicar's sermon, or he may choose
to modify the fabric of the verse itself. The impersonal
stimulus to the imagination ends once the new thoughts
have been called into existence.

To Auden the attempt to write freely and naturally in
a poem, as Romantic theories of art would have him do,
is the most certain way to avoid true self-discovery or self-

[52] "A Literary Transference," 85. For an example of how far
Auden is willing to go in accepting the gift of pure accident, see
Letters from Iceland, 27, where he prefers the mistaken reading of
"ports" for the original "poets" in line two of "Journey to Iceland,"
CP, 7.

revelation. He finds both poet and reader all too willing to suspend their disbelief in the poetic world of verbal magic. Only the luck of playing in form and technique can possibly trick either reader or writer into discovering new insight in a poem.

CHAPTER VI

OPERA:
THE RAKE'S PROGRESS

To one sort of literary critic, the opera seems such a frivolous genre that close attention to it betrays undue critical solemnity. On the other hand, to anyone who follows the lead of Auden's deprecating remarks about a libretto's lack of artistic autonomy, such a work may seem unsuited to independent literary analysis. Indeed, to evaluate a libretto as poetry outside the operatic composite would be unfair. I propose simply to analyze the libretto to *The Rake's Progress* as a poem which happens to conform to the requirements of opera, just as *For the Time Being* accepts the basic limitations of oratorio. Taken as an operatic poem, *The Rake's Progress* exemplifies in a simplified and clear form those qualities which this study has found to be most characteristic of Auden's mature poetic mode. This initial impression is reaffirmed by a close examination of the libretto, despite its dual authorship.

In *The Rake's Progress* (and two succeeding libretti), Chester Kallman played an important role as Auden's collaborator. To separate their individual contributions is ultimately impossible because their joint efforts have produced a cohesive work of art as end product. In addition, their collaboration draws on a close and mutually stimulating friendship of many years standing. Monroe Spears has formulated what is probably the most sensible assessment of Kallman's contribution that one can make,[1]

[1] *Poetry of Auden*, 270-272. Though prepared independently, this

but the collaborators seem quite right in describing their work as subject to a "corporate personality."[2] To the analysis I propose, the authorship of particular passages is essentially irrelevant. The Auden-Kallman *Rake's Progress* as it stands is, in however simplified a fashion, both poetic and dramatic. Analysis can show how its plan and many devices of its execution are exemplary of Auden's work as a whole.

Auden's progressive involvement with opera deserves some preliminary attention. When he first encountered Italian opera in the late 1930's, Auden was frequently collaborating with Benjamin Britten in song cycles.[3] Shortly after coming to America, the two decided to try their talents at a "school opera." *Paul Bunyan* was performed briefly at Columbia University in 1941, but the authors rejected it as unsuccessful and declined publication.[4] A reading of the mimeographed libretto convinces me that they were entirely right and that this experiment throws little light on Auden's more mature work in opera. Through the next decade Auden's competence in opera increased rapidly and, particularly since World War II, he has devoted a significant portion of his creative energy to writing, translating, and theorizing about operas. His

---

chapter necessarily has many similarities to Mr. Spears's analytical summary of *The Rake's Progress*, pp. 269-278.

[2] *DH*, 482. This recent statement seems to minimize the importance of the official division of credit between Auden and Kallman, published by Alan Ansen, Auden's private secretary from 1948-1953. See "A Communication," *Hudson Review*, IX (Spring 1956), 319-320.

[3] See *Making, Knowing, and Judging*, 12. *DH*, 40. For Auden's work with Britten, see Edward Callan, *Annotated Checklist*, Nos. 39-51. No. 52 appears to be based on mistaken information since Auden reports no recollection of any music by Britten for *For the Time Being*.

[4] Monroe Spears gives a useful summary in *Poetry of Auden*, 265-269.

high appraisal of the genre is evident in his judgment
that the golden age of European opera (Gluck's *Orpheus*
to Verdi's *Otello*) surpasses in greatness the seventy-five
years of Greek tragedy.[5] The last ten years have seen two
new Auden-Kallman libretti: "Delia, or A Masque of
Night" and *Elegy for Young Lovers*.[6] Auden and Kallman
have also translated and adapted into English two Mozart
operas, *The Magic Flute* and *Don Giovanni,* and Brecht-
Weill's *Seven Deadly Sins*.[7] In addition, Auden has
seemed sufficiently expert for the Radio Corporation of
America to use program notes by him for a number of
opera recordings.[8]

Out of this considerable association with the genre,
Auden has formulated a conception of the nature and
value of opera which can provide a useful background to
this study of *The Rake's Progress.* He developed his
theory of opera in a number of poems and critical articles,
most of them written about the time of the first performance of *The Rake* in 1951. For the purposes of exposition,
Auden's conception of opera may be divided into two
complementary facets: the artifice of opera and its moral
realism.

As suggested earlier, a major value of opera for Auden
is its high artifice. The obviously artificial conventions

---

[5] "Introduction," to *The Portable Greek Reader* (New York,
1948), 7.

[6] See, respectively, *Botteghe Oscure,* XII (1953), 164-210, and the
libretto published by B. Schott's Sons (Mainz, West Germany,
1961). Spears effectively summarizes both in *Poetry of Auden,*
278-288.

[7] The Mozart libretti were published separately in 1956 and
1961 respectively. The Brecht translation appears in *Tulane Drama
Review,* VI (September 1961), 123-129.

[8] See, for example, "Verismo Opera," in George Marek, ed.,
The World Treasury of Grand Opera (New York, 1956), 142-148.
DH, 475-482.

which govern the genre will presumably restrain viewers from responding to the world of an opera too literally. The music is a dominant force for intensifying artifice. In some types of poetry for music, like lyrics and chants, the music is subordinate to the dictates of the words, but in song Auden, following Mozart, believes "the notes must be free to be whatever they choose and the words must be able to do what they are told. . . . The verses which the librettist writes are not addressed to the public but are really a private letter to the composer."[9] In the case of *The Rake's Progress*, cooperation between composer and the librettists seems to have been carried on with just the kind of subordination of words to music that Auden describes. Igor Stravinsky says of the collaboration: "Auden amazed me with his applied poetic skill. He performed prodigies of versification by maneuvering the order of a few simple words."[10] For Auden's conception of the musician who will manipulate the poet's words, we can turn to a poem entitled "The Composer" (1940):

> All the others translate: the painter sketches
> A visible world to love or reject;
> Rummaging into his living, the poet fetches
> The images out that hurt and connect.
>
> From Life to Art by painstaking adaption,
> Relying on us to cover the rift;

[9] "Some Reflections on Opera as a Medium," *Tempo* [London], No. 20 (Summer 1951), 9. *DH*, 472-473.

[10] "A Statement by the Composer," on insert accompanying Columbia recording of *The Rake's Progress*, No. SL-125. For a fuller account of the collaboration from the composer's point of view, see *Memories and Commentaries*, by Igor Stravinsky with Robert Craft (New York, 1960).

> Only your notes are pure contraption,
> Only your song is an absolute gift.[11]

As we have seen, Auden's poetry by itself tends to emphasize its own verbal contrivance; the "pure contraption" of music can only heighten the artifice.

The visual dimension of operatic stagecraft, to Auden, occupies a subordinate position. At best, it can reinforce artifice by avoiding verisimilitude.

> In opera the Heard and the Seen are like Reality and Appearance in philosophy; hence the more frankly theatrical and sham the sets the better. Good taste is not in order. . . . Only one thing is essential, namely, that everything be a little over life size, that the stage be a space in which only the grand entrance and the grand gesture are appropriate.[12]

Similarly, Auden welcomes the apparent incongruities of casting created by the physical corpulence of many opera singers. To have lovers sung by overweight "Wagnerians" reiterates visually the fact that operatic love is not motivated by physical attractiveness.

A more important aspect of the operatic composite is drama—an imitation of human action. As drama, opera properly deals in simplified characters and improbable plots:

> All good drama has two movements, first the making of the mistake, then the discovery that it was a mistake. . . . [The librettist] is more limited in the kinds of mistakes he can use. . . . Self-deception is impossible in opera because music is immediate, not reflective;

[11] *CP*, 5.
[12] "Some Reflections on Opera," 9.

whatever is sung is the case. . . . The drama of recognition [of the mistake] must be tropically abrupt, for music cannot exist in an atmosphere of uncertainty.[13]

Once self-deception and indecision are banned, psychologically complex characters are impossible. What opera does emphasize about human nature is passion and emotional self-assertion. Hence there is a limited kind of plot appropriate to a libretto. As Auden sees his job, the librettist necessarily deals in melodramatic improbabilities:

> A credible situation in opera means a situation in which it is credible that someone should sing. . . . It offers as many opportunities as possible for the characters to be swept off their feet by placing them in situations which are too tragic or too fantastic for "words." No good opera plot can be sensible for people do not sing when they are feeling sensible.[14]

The improbable plot with its simplified characters and their inflated emotional states is, in fact, one of the sources of greatest annoyance to those who reject opera. But Auden sees these characteristics of the genre as assets to be exploited for their ability to project archetypal or mythical situations, which are universally human by nature. Opera's obvious departure from realistic or, to use Auden's term, "documentary," presentation of life frees it to dramatize such timeless situations directly, as in a morality play.

Auden's conception of the drama of opera is strikingly reminiscent of the dramatic theory he developed while writing his own plays. We recall that in 1935 Auden called for characters that were "simplified, easily recognizable

---

[13] *Ibid.*, 8. Adapted in *DH*, 471.
[14] *Ibid.*, 8-9. *DH*, 471-472, with slight revisions.

and over life-size," and dramatic speech with "the same self-confessed, significant and undocumentary character as dramatic movement." The drama he conceived at that time was to deal with the general and universal, as opposed to the particular and local.[15] Opera by its very nature can fulfill all these requirements. Instead of requiring a new conception of drama, then, opera provides a medium to which Auden's instinctive dramatic bent is uniquely appropriate.

The artifice of opera involves music, language, visual effects, simplified characters, and melodramatic plot. The other main emphasis of Auden's theory—his insistence on the realism of opera—is more unexpected. He proposes that the opera, which is so obviously and inescapably "performed," is itself an accurate figure for the moral essence of human life as he has come to understand it. His earliest suggestion that life is as fantastic as opera comes in "The Sea and the "Mirror" where Caliban is probing the dramatist's, or in more general terms, the artist's problems in creating an effective metaphor for human existence.

> Beating about for some large loose image to define the original drama which aroused his imitative passion, the first performance in which the players were their own audience, the worldly stage on which their behaving flesh was really sore and sorry—for the floods of tears were not caused by onions, the deformities and wounds did not come off after a good wash, the self-stabbed heroine could not pick herself up again to make a gracious bow nor her seducer go demurely home to his

[15] See above, p. 99. Quotations from "What I want the theatre to be," as reported in Ashley Dukes, "The English Scene," *Theatre Arts*, xix (December 1935), 907-908.

plain and middle-aged spouse—the fancy immediately flushed is of the greatest grandest opera rendered by a very provincial touring company indeed.[16]

This passage, rich not only in rhetoric but in telling particulars, opens Auden's description of life as opera. Human beings are simultaneously the ham actors and the audience who, in conscience, must refuse to applaud their own "indescribably inexcusably awful" performance. Thus the theater becomes a summarizing figure for the double nature of man: As human beings, we not only act, but are self-consciously aware of our acting. When the performance is over (symbolically, at the point of death), "We do at last see ourselves as we are, neither cozy nor playful, but swaying out on the ultimate wind-whipped cornice that overhangs the unabiding void—we have never stood anywhere else,—when our reasons are silenced by the heavy huge derision,—There is nothing to say." At this point, when he gives up the words he has relied on to deceive and to display himself, man is open to intuitions of the realm of Being beyond the human theater-world we all inhabit. We can then perceive the existence of "that Wholly Other Life from which we are separated by an essential emphatic gulf of which our contrived fissures of mirror and proscenium arch . . . are feebly figurative signs."

In a theater the proscenium arch separates the imagined world (Ariel's) that the characters inhabit from the everyday world (Caliban's) which the spectators represent. The work of art on stage both imitates and judges the everyday world. As human beings, however, we can also, by a leap of negative knowledge (see above, p. 118),

[16] CP, 401.

conceive imaginatively of the realm of ultimate Being, which is the moral ground for judging the whole human theater of existence. From this cosmic religious perspective, humanity appears as a group of shoddy performers indeed. The work of art, then, in its "feebly figurative" way, captures in its contrivance and artifice the "incorrigible staginess" of human life seen from the perspective of the Eternal. The most fantastic form of art, the opera, can portray human life most "realistically" in its exaggerated dramatization of human posturing.

By the time of *The Rake's Progress* a few years later, Auden had defined the realism of opera more specifically. The essentially operatic characteristic of humanity, he concludes, is emotional willfulness. Auden finds that at life's crucial moments human beings cling to emotional fixations, no matter how inappropriate to the living situation. These gratuitous and willfully asserted emotions are the source of man's greatest moments and his worst. A person's response to opera, Auden predicts, will depend on how central he believes such emotional willfulness to be in human nature:

> If . . . you believe that human beings are most characteristically human, as contrasted with any other creature, when they are doing something just for the hell of it, or that all men are constantly adopting some emotion and defending it with the same intense energy as that with which the characters in a Shavian play adopt and defend some point of view. . . , then all the usual objections of the opera hater . . . will seem to you not objections but advantages of the medium. . . .
>
> [One might say:] "What psychological insight to construct so many plots around one or the other of the

two most uniquely human acts, laying down one's life for one's friend and cutting off one's nose to spite one's face. How realistic to show that, whatever it may be in between, life at its best and its worst is a *performance* that defies common sense."[17]

The moral realism of opera, its inherent propensity to display the willfulness in human nature, correlates with Auden's view that music cannot project psychological uncertainty. If operatic humanity cannot express self-doubt, then it must, perforce, be able to assert itself willfully.

Since Auden developed his operatic theory partly on the basis of his experience with *The Rake's Progress*, this work very predictably follows the major outlines of his theory. Willfulness is a major factor in its theme: that through suffering or facing death, we must learn Love and unlearn the willfully egocentric self-deceptions men are born with. In developing this theme, *The Rake's Progress*, instead of cultivating a grand manner for its own sake, turns the artifice of opera to emphasize its moral realism. There are fantastic episodes, like the marriage of the protagonist to a bearded lady from the circus, but these are presented as manifestations of the willful self-seeking of the focal character, Tom Rakewell. The asides of Nick Shadow, his "servant," early remind the audience that Tom is the dupe of the devil and, even more, of himself. As a result, the spectator can see the fantastic less as a property of the operatic world as a whole and more as the aberration of Tom.

While the character of Tom Rakewell is of central importance in articulating the theme of the opera, the struc-

[17] "Opera Addict," *Vogue*, cxii (July 1948), 65, 101.

ture through which his progress is developed deserves particular comment. By conventional standards, there is not a plot, but a series of pictures of the state of Tom's mind at different times. The lack of plot allows the librettists to avoid specifying what motivates Tom as an individual.

> Though a single picture defines the relations between its component figures, a story told in a succession of pictures is a succession of static tableaux in which the present supersedes the past; what is portrayed in one picture is not the cause of what is portrayed in the next but is merely previous to it.[18]

With the lack of a cause-and-effect relation between successive scenes, Tom Rakewell must seem self-motivated in the sense of being motivated by his fallen nature as a human being. Once the audience has accepted Tom's actions as "natural" for a human being, they have, in effect, recognized him as a representative figure for everyman. The succession of tableaux is especially appropriate in opera, because it provides for interruptions in the flow of action for the sake of arias and ensembles. In addition, this structure, like the similar progressions in Auden's semi-dramas and plays, focuses primary attention on states of mind rather than on specific individuals. Particularly in Auden's plays the tableau structure was less than successful in developing convincing dramatic character. In opera, where the effectiveness of the whole does not depend so much on forceful characters, a series of static pictures is entirely appropriate and can be, as in the case at hand, highly effective.

[18] "The Rake's Progress," *Harper's Bazaar*, LXXXVII (February 1953), 165.

The first tableau of the opera places an eighteenth-century Tom Rakewell and his Anne Trulove in her father's garden on a spring afternoon. The two share a childishly innocent love, as their duet emphasizes by poetically relocating them in a paradisal garden presided over by a pastoral Venus:

Anne: With fragrant odours and with notes of cheer
       The pious earth observes the solemn year.
Tom: Now is the season when the Cyprian Queen
       With genial charm translates our mortal scene,
       When swains their nymphs in fervent arms
         enfold
       And with a kiss restore the Age of Gold.[19]

The lovers' vision of eternal bliss is, in a Kierkegaardian sense, aesthetic. Their pastoral springtime imagery emphasizes their failure to accept the limitations of human existence in time. By postulating a world of pure ideal, they preclude, for the space of this brief scene, the inevitable ethical conflict between natural desire and moral duty. Hence the garden Tom and Anne appear in is analogous to Eden and they are comparable to Adam and Eve before the Fall.

The aria which follows, sung by Tom alone, signals his Fall, for it reveals how his inflated self-importance unfits him for the true love offered by Anne Trulove. He refuses the offer of a job from his prospective father-in-law because of the self-discipline "the drudge's yoke" would require. A

[19] *The Rake's Progress*, Vocal Score (New York, 1951), 3-4. Further page references to this edition will be included in the text in parentheses. Repetitions of words necessitated by the music have been deleted. For one of Auden's many discussions of the conflict between natural desire and moral duty, see *The Enchafèd Flood*, especially pp. 28-30.

heretic akin to Marlowe's Faustus, he acts as if he lived in a wish-world where the lucky are rich and hence happy. In the Kierkegaardian perspective he commits the prototypical Romantic error of denying that he is a fallen creature subject to ethical demands. He attempts to live aesthetically as if luck were more important than goodness.

> Have not grave doctors assured us that good works are of no avail for heaven predestines all? In my fashion I may profess myself of their party and herewith entrust myself to Fortune.

> > Since it is not by merit
> > We rise or we fall,
> > But the favour of Fortune
> > That governs us all,
> > Why should I labour
> > For what in the end
> > She will give me for nothing
> > If she be my friend?
> > . . . .
> > My life lies before me,
> > The world is so wide:
> > Come, wishes, be horses;
> > This beggar shall ride. (12-14)

The reorientation of a maxim ("If wishes were horses, then beggars would ride") is, as we have seen, one of Auden's favorite light-verse devices (see above, p. 134, for an earlier use of the same maxim). The members of any opera audience could be expected to recognize the adage on which Tom draws. They should also perceive that his resolution of the conditional form of the maxim is a sign for his egoism and his incipient degeneration.

In response to Tom's wish that he had money, the ominous Nick Shadow appears with news that "an uncle" has left him a fortune. Tom is too overjoyed to question the curious promptness of his good fortune and engages Nick as a servant who can show him the proper style of behavior for a rich man. Tom naïvely accepts this devil's pact that in a year and a day he shall pay "no more and no less than what you yourself acknowledge to be just" (30). Shadow is not, however, corrupting a previously innocent man; Tom is the source of his own degradation, as is re-emphasized when all express their gratitude for the bequest. Anne Trulove and her father thank Heaven for this gift; Tom treats his wealth as evidence of the power his wishes have over Fate (20-21). As the scene ends, Nick opens the gate of the garden and the two lovers pass through it into the world of adult life.

Nick openly reveals himself as a devil by announcing to the audience that the progress of a rake is beginning. The spectators are now certain that Tom is making a serious mistake, but he himself will not discover his error until he is faced with death and judgment. This dramatic irony, which frames the action of the opera until Nick comes to collect his just due in Act III, places the audience in a position of superior judgment from which they can condemn Tom. The librettists, however, carefully develop Tom's progress to emphasize the ways in which he is simply fulfilling the instinctive hedonism of human nature. Thus Nick Shadow seems more a personification of Tom's—and every man's—willful self-indulgence than a real devil. Nick need only assist the natural man in fulfilling his fallen nature.

Nick's first act of assistance is to introduce Tom to some of his fellow human creatures in a London brothel presided over by, startlingly enough, Mother Goose. A chorus of whores and roaring boys express their devotion to the twin gods of human desire, Venus and Mars. Here again, their degeneration is essentially human. The roaring boys, for example, sing: "For what is sweeter to human nature/ Than to quarrel over nothing at all" (38-39). The references to Venus in the whores' song provide an ironic contrast with the Venus of the paradisal garden, for this goddess, who goes under the same name, embodies love as purely physical, sensual *eros*.

In the brothel Nick, now Tom's "godfather," catechizes him in "the delights to which your newly found state of manhood is about to call you" (42). Tom swears dutifully:

> One aim in all things to pursue:
> My duty to myself to do. . . .
> To shut my ears to prude and preacher
> And follow Nature as my teacher (43).

Nature here clearly refers to the unredeemed human nature which leads men to seek pleasure as opposed to love and duty. Continuing his catechism, Tom balks only at repeating Nick's secularized definition of love, thereby indicating that he has not entirely forgotten Anne. However, Nick persuades him to continue with his initiation into "humanhood" by turning back the clock from one a.m. to midnight. That Tom should believe that time can be turned back is palpably absurd; yet probably every human being would have to admit that he at some time either believed or wanted to believe Nick's rationalization of his trick: "See. Time is yours. The hours obey your pleasure./ Fear not. Enjoy. You may repent at leisure."[20]

[20] *The Rake's Progress*, 47. This speech recalls another old saw: "Marry in haste; repent at leisure."

Tom's song of initiation is a poignant expression of his lingering awareness that he is betraying Anne Trulove, yet his response to the song only re-emphasizes his willful refusal to do what he knows is right.

> Love, my sorrow and my shame,
> *Though thou daily be forgot,*
> Goddess, *O forget me not.*
> Lest I perish, O be nigh
> In my darkest hour that I,
>   Dying, dying,
> May call upon thy sacred name.[21]

Tom knows he is doing wrong yet cannot bring himself to treat that fact seriously—to repent and amend his life. Shortly afterwards, Tom is led upstairs by Mother Goose.

The third scene of this first act finds Anne, conscious of having been forgotten, but true to her love, answering Tom's song: "Love hears, Love knows,/ Love answers him across the silent miles, and goes" (61). With overtones of Shakespeare's Sonnet 116 Anne's aria reasserts the Love that has its analogue in heaven.

The first tableau of Act II expresses Tom's condition of heart at an indeterminately later time. The librettists again emphasize Tom's willfulness by putting in his mouth a thorough condemnation of the life he has been leading:

> O Nature, green unnatural mother, how I have followed where you led. Is it for this I left the country? No ploughman is more a slave to sun, moon and season than a gentleman to the clock of fashion (73-74).

In answer to his own question, born of disgust of himself and the world around him, "Who's honest, chaste, or

21 *The Rake's Progress*, 51-52; my italics.

kind?" he replies, "One, only one, and of her I dare not think" (75-76). Once again, the only apparent reason he has for not daring to think of Anne is that to recognize her he would have to change his self-indulgent mode of living. Instead, he resigns himself once more to the self-defeating hunt for novelty and pleasure, even while recognizing its futility in a wistful wish for happiness.

Seeing his master's weariness, Nick Shadow offers a new suggestion for achieving happiness. Since the multitudes of men are driven by either appetite or conscience, Nick proposes that Tom act "freely":

> For he alone is free
> Who chooses what to will and wills
> His choice as destiny.
> No eye his future can foretell,
> No law his past explain
> Whom neither passion can compel
> Nor reason restrain (85-86).

St. Augustine probably was the first to define this corrupted notion of freedom for Auden.[22] The episode is, in effect, a satirical thrust at the *acte gratuit* as described by atheistic existentialists like Sartre. Tom accepts Nick's suggestion of an entirely "free" act by deciding to marry Baba, the bearded Turk from St. Giles Fair. The fundamental absurdity of this action lies in the unfulfilling nature of what his self-will leads him to seek; this marriage is foredoomed by the very grounds that lead Tom to choose it. Tom once more expresses his self-absorption by savoring the notoriety that will be his for wooing, wedding, and bedding this prodigy of nature (87-91).

Just as Tom is about to bring Baba home after their

---

[22] See "Squares and Oblongs," 167.

wedding, Anne arrives at his house to open scene two. In the prose of her recitative Anne expresses some self-doubt which has the dramatically valuable effect of humanizing her near-perfect dedication to Love: "Although the heart for love dare everything, the hand draws back and finds no spring of courage" (95). This psychological complexity, however, still conforms to Auden's theory that music cannot project uncertainty, for her aria, which is sung, reaffirms her unqualified faith that "A love that is sworn before Thee [Heaven] can plunder hell of its prey" (97-98). Confronted with Anne as he brings Baba home, Tom can only send her away, recalling the springtime of their love and expressing the winter that is now in his heart. After Baba has displayed her fabled beard, thus emphasizing visually the absurdity of Tom's "free" act, her character is developed into a delightful satiric portrait of a tourist fondling her knickknacks. Driven to distraction by her prattle, Tom jams his wig over her head, cutting off the final run of her aria (124). He seeks the only remedy left to relieve his self-willed frustration—sleep.

One more satiric tableau demonstrates how the rake embodies the tendencies of every man. While Tom sleeps, Nick demonstrates a ridiculous false-bottomed machine which appears to produce bread from broken glass. The audience is to see clearly that the machine is a crude fake. When Tom sees in it the embodiment of what he has just been dreaming, he is obviously guilty of fantastic credulity. But the vision Tom proceeds to unfold has been the hope of innumerable utopians, liberal humanists, and believers in human progress:

> Thanks to this excellent device
> Man shall re-enter paradise

From which he once was driven.
Secure from need, the cause of crime,
The world shall for the second time
Be similar to heaven.

. . . .

Omnipotent when armed with this,
In secular abundant bliss
He shall ascend the Chain
Of Being to its top to win
The throne of Nature and begin
His everlasting reign (130-135).

Tom falls for so transparent a device to bring about the
"secular abundant bliss" that the audience must assent to
Nick's satiric aside: "There's no fantastic lie/ You cannot
make men swallow if you try" (133). On the other hand,
Romantic quests for a heaven on earth are by no means
uncommon in the mid-twentieth century. The audience,
on reflection, may recognize that they share Tom's basic
impulse. If they take this step, they will discover that
they have been drawn into self-mockery in laughing at
Tom.

Act III opens with an auction of Tom's effects after
the promotion of his bread machine has ruined him.
The chatter of the greedy and rapacious auction crowd in-
forms us that "hundreds of sober merchants" (143) have
also been taken in by Tom's machine out of their desire
for profit rather than any foolish altruism like Tom's
desire to be the savior of mankind. Sellem, the auctioneer,
produces a rationale for auctions that implicitly condemns
misplaced missionary zeal as much as profiteering.

Truly there is a divine balance in Nature: a thousand
lose that a thousand may gain; and you who are the

fortunate are not so only in yourselves, but also in being
Nature's missionaries. You are her instruments for the
restoration of that order we all so worship, and it is
granted to, ah! so few of us to serve (151-152).

Sellem is a most successful auctioneer because he knows
the proper temptation to hold out to human nature: the
possibility that owning this particular material object
"may be salvation" (162). The last object to be sold is
Baba, still stifled with Tom's wig. When it is removed, she
first finishes her interrupted trill before voicing her annoyance with the officious curiosity of the crowd. The
scene ends with Baba charitably relinquishing Tom to
Anne, who is still searching for him. Baba herself announces a return to the stage as her "self-indulgent inter-
mezzo ends" (174).

Immediately thereafter (Act III, Scene 2), Tom's self-
indulgence is also brought to an end. Nick Shadow leads
him, now penniless, to a graveyard. A year and a day have
passed and Nick is out to collect his wages—Tom's soul.
Nick resolves the dramatic irony that has been in effect
since his entrance into the opera by revealing to Tom that
he is, in fact, a devil. After Tom implores Heaven for
mercy, Nick relents from his demand that Tom commit
suicide at the stroke of midnight and, to toy with him,
offers a chance at survival. If Tom will name correctly
three successive cards Nick cuts from a deck, he will be
freed. A significant *double-entendre* in Nick's baiting suggests to Tom the way to guess the first card correctly.
Nick, speaking of cards, suggests, "Let wish be thought
and think on one to name" (195). Tom does think on
one to name—Anne. In the strength of his conviction that
she is his only source of help in the face of death, Tom

[173]

names the Queen of Hearts, the first card. An apparent
accident aids Tom on the second card. A sudden noise
startles him into a mild oath, "The deuce!" (199); turning, he sees that a spade used to dig his grave has fallen
over. Again trusting that Anne is behind him, he correctly
identifies the two of spades. For the third card Nick slyly
reinserts the Queen of Hearts after appearing to have
thrown it away. Calling again on Love, Tom hears Anne's
voice off stage and, trusting Love over the evidence of his
senses, correctly reiterates the Queen of Hearts. Nick sinks
back to Hell, but only after condemning Tom to insanity
as punishment for his sins.

This important scene, in dramatic terms the recognition of the mistake, has been read as Anne's saving of
Tom.[23] More precisely, Tom is saved by his newfound
willingness to have faith in her as an embodiment of Love.
Anne, whose name means "grace," has exhibited a nearly
angelic dedication in searching for Tom, but her efforts
accomplish nothing without his realization in the face of
death that the Love she bears is his only source for hope.
In this scene the one line she sings from off stage, reiterating that a love sworn before Heaven can plunder Hell
of its prey, indicates not her physical presence, but Tom's
conscious recognition of what she has been singing all the
time. Of course, without an Anne Trulove in whom he
could recover faith, he would certainly be lost, but his recognition of her is the new element in this scene which
saves him.

The final scene of the opera proper, Tom in Bedlam,
has been more seriously misunderstood.[24] In the immediate

[23] See Joseph Kerman, *Opera as Drama* (New York, 1956), 246.
[24] See, for example, Kerman, 246-247. Mr. Kerman's reading
on this point seems a minor flaw in a thoughtful analysis.

dramatic situation, Anne pays a lover's visit to the asylum where Tom in his madness conceives of himself as Adonis. But symbolically she is a Heavenly Venus bringing a message of grace and redemption to a repentant sinner. At the end of the scene Anne returns to her normal human self regretfully acknowledging that the love she and Tom share cannot be consummated on earth:

> Every wearied body must
> Late or soon return to dust,
> Set the frantic spirit free.
> In this earthly city we
> Shall not meet again, love, yet
> Never think that I forget.[25]

Within the scene the characters and the setting itself undergo a vital symbolic transformation, which is accomplished primarily by the poetry. Bedlam is unmistakably portrayed as a hell on earth by the chorus of madmen; with echoes of Dante ("Leave all love and hope behind" [212]), they locate Bedlam below the earthly city in a place where there are no marriages, no ranks of society, and no light. The madmen are still human and hence actors, but they are less than fully human, for each is limited to a single role—Tom's that of Adonis, the human lover of a goddess. However, the librettists differentiate Tom from the others by exploring the paradoxes possible in the word "madness." Tom and the chorus each accuse the other of being "mad" (227-228), and both are, but in different senses of the word. Tom has that form of earth's

---

[25] *The Rake's Progress*, 225-226. The libretto distributed with the Columbia recording of the opera has, instead of "frantic spirit," "*homesick* spirit," a reading which, though less easily sung to a quarter and an eighth note, would preserve another echo of Augustine's *Confessions* (Book 1).

madness which is Heaven's sense; he understands himself in relation to the transcendent reality of Anne as the Heavenly Venus. The chorus, on the other hand, can only lament the loss of the earthly life from which they are now cut off by insanity (212-213). Tom in his madness has returned to a state of childlike irresponsibility similar to that in the paradisal garden at the opera's beginning, but there is an important difference. Having faced death in the graveyard, he has learned that only Love can redeem a life of self-indulgence. He can now see that his former life was itself a kind of worldly madness, difficult to recognize because it is the norm of human behavior. Having committed himself to faith in Love with his last act of responsible choice, he now longs for only one thing—that Love shall reassure him that he is not forgotten.

Into the darkness of Bedlam comes Anne, assuming the role of the Angel-Goddess of Love, Venus. Tom as Adonis, voicing the repentance implicit in calling on Anne in the graveyard scene, confesses his sins to Venus. He repents his former madness in living the life of earthly pleasures; he has awakened from that dream to the transcendent Reality of a Heavenly Love. She pardons him, saying, "the wild boar is vanquished" (219).

In the mythical story, the wild boar embodies Adonis' pursuit of earthly pleasure in hunting, for which he is willing to leave the immortal love of Venus. In Tom's case the hunt for the boar has been his quest after the pleasures of a rake. The boar causes Adonis' death and, in the implied parallel, the destruction of Tom's sanity; but in Anne's reassurance that the boar is conquered lies the promise that death has been vanquished for Tom, that his spirit is assured of salvation. Venus and Adonis have

a brief duet celebrating their spiritual union in an eternal
Now:

> Rejoice, beloved: in these fields of Elysium
> Space cannot alter, nor time our love abate;
> Here has no words for Absence or Estrangement
> Nor Now a notion of Almost or Too Late.[26]

Tom, however, unlike Anne as Angel-Venus, is still
mortal and his body weakens: "Immortal queen, permit
thy mortal bridegroom to lay his head upon thy breast./
The Heavens are merciful, and all is well" (221). Anne
sings him to sleep with a beautiful aria which even the
chorus of madmen recognizes as the "sacred music of the
spheres" (223). The first stanza sufficiently conveys its
promise of a heavenly paradise for his soul:

> Gently, little boat,
> Across the waters float,
> Their crystal waves dividing;
>> The sun in the west
>> Is going to rest:
>>> Glide, glide, glide,
> Toward the Islands of the Blest.[27]

Tom wakes after Anne's departure still hoping for an
earthly consummation for his love, but, on finding his
Venus gone, he dies. The opera proper closes with a
moving dirge for Adonis, but the preceding encounter
between Venus and Adonis makes it clear that the chorus
mourns only for the body of Adonis; his soul will be re-
born in paradise.

[26] *The Rake's Progress*, 220-221. See earlier discussion of capitalization in Auden's poetry, pp. 84-85.

[27] *The Rake's Progress*, 222, here quoted in the form established
in *The Shield of Achilles*, 49.

After the final curtain the major actors suddenly reappear, the men without wigs and Baba without her beard, to sing an epilogue. Its operatic precedents are Mozart's *Don Giovanni* and Weill-Brecht's *The Three-Penny Opera*,[28] and in accordance with that tradition its ostensible function is to point the moral of the fable:

Anne: Not every rake is rescued
At the last by Love and Beauty;
Not every man
Is given an Anne
To take the place of Duty. . . .
Tom: Beware, young men who fancy
You are Virgil or Julius Caesar,
Lest when you wake
You be only a rake. . . .
All: For idle hands
And hearts and minds
The Devil finds
A work, dear Sir, fair Madam,
For you and you (233-240).

Besides echoing, in matter and manner, the sermonizing conclusions to morality plays, this epilogue also functions like one of Auden's Janus-jokes. The moralizing is set in witty, artificial and rather quaint verse and is sung by actors who are partly out of costume; hence the epilogue can be a source of amusement for a sophisticated modern audience. Yet on its serious side, the epilogue helps to shatter whatever artistic illusion the audience may have come to accept as "real" and reminds them that what

[28] Mr. Auden reports that he saw the first performance of *Die Dreigroschenoper* in Berlin, August 31, 1928. Brecht and Weill were adapting John Gay's *The Beggar's Opera*, which is thus another eighteenth-century precedent for Auden.

they have seen and heard is an artistic contraption. One might think that no such device for insisting on a clear distinction between art and life would be necessary in the case of such an obviously artificial genre as opera, but a quotation from one of the many critical attacks on this epilogue can illustrate just how "seriously" spectators can take the world of the work of art once they have accepted the conventions which establish it:

> What Stravinsky has written, to these words, means one thing—that Tom Rakewell is dead of a broken heart. The audience is touched in a way it never is in "Don Giovanni," and when composer and librettist try to laugh if off in a gay little epilogue they merely wound the audience's feelings without convincing them that it was all make-believe.[29]

The assumption of this commentator that he should respond to art as if it were a pleasantly sentimental version of life provides a remarkable echo of the audience's views in "The Sea and the Mirror."[30] Both would prefer art to remain a self-contained world in which one can be "touched" without reminders of the real unpleasantness of actual life, where no one dies of a broken heart. Auden's counter-insistence, dramatized in the epilogue to *The Rake*, is that no audience should be allowed to leave the theater without a reminder of the radical difference between the play world of art and the real world in which their lives need rectification. The annoyance expressed in critical comments like the one quoted suggests that for some viewers the epilogue struck home with its intended result.

[29] Colin Mason, "Stravinsky's Opera," *Music and Letters*, XXXIII (January 1952), 8. See also Kerman, 247.
[30] See *CP*, 377-378.

The epilogue makes explicit the didactic focusing of the opera, which has been implicit all along in the treatment of Tom as an everyman, but the opera's Audenesque brand of didacticism becomes especially evident when the opera is compared with the series of eighteenth-century prints by William Hogarth which suggested the title, the setting, and the scenes in the brothel and Bedlam. Where Hogarth is consistent in satirically condemning his rake, the librettists create a character who is never vicious and is frequently sympathetic in his inability to overcome his willful pleasure-seeking. Tom's sentiments and desires are those of a majority of human beings. His attempts to avoid the ultimately moral or religious dimensions of human existence are cast in terms that any audience might well recognize as their own: the wish for material wealth, the craving to be a free agent, and the desire to make a heaven on earth. The dramatic irony created by the fact that the audience, but not Tom, see that Nick is a devil, makes it possible for them to condemn the rake; on the other hand, the fact that Tom expresses their own desires and ambitions deftly leads them toward self-condemnation.

The dramatic structure which presents Tom's character is not only appropriate to and successful for its genre, but also, as we have noted, characteristic of Auden's earlier dramatic productions. The succession of tableaux is particularly useful in the opera, for our interest is properly focused on the state of mind of the character who has stopped the action in order to sing out his feelings. As suggested earlier, the tableau structure is ill-suited to presenting continuous growth of dramatic character; predictably, Tom's character shows a minimum of development. As Auden outlined in his theory of opera, there are only two essential parts to the dramatic movement: Tom makes his humanly natural mistake and abruptly recognizes it as an error when he is confronted with death. Once Tom has left the garden he does not become significantly more degenerate, except in the limited sense that he willfully refuses to repent after each of his foolish wishes. The tableau structure is limited to presenting static states of character, but its compensating advantage is that any scene may transform the perspective in which we see and judge character. In *The Rake* the Bedlam scene serves just such a function: it presents Tom as a repentant and faithful Adonis, receiving a visit from Anne, now transformed into a personification of Grace. This sudden change in the terms of the dramatic action makes the opera similar to *The Ascent of F6*. There, the dramatic action per se ends with Michael's collapse near the summit of the mountain, but symbolic action continues through several tableaux which probe the significance of his climb. The Bedlam scene provides an analogous break in the dramatic action for the sake of symbolically important action. In this respect *The Rake's Progress* is more successful than its prototype among Auden's works, for it introduces the symbolic transformation in a setting that is dramatically motivated: Bedlam is the logical place for Tom as a madman, and words and action that might seem absurd in a normal human context are easily accepted in an insane asylum.

The Bedlam scene is also important for its allegorical transformation of Anne into the ambassador of Heavenly Love. We have seen already how Tom is developed into an allegorical everyman, but Anne's transmutation is even more deftly handled. Up to this scene she has had a human stature, though her prayerful dedication to Love might be described as saintly in its fortitude. However, in visiting Tom, she assumes the role of Venus, ostensibly to humor his particular aberration that he is Adonis. Then, out of this perfectly motivated pose, she sings words that could come only from a forgiving Heaven. Once her message of Grace has been delivered, her father, himself a transparent allegorical figure for Duty, calls her back to human stature.

The poetry which assists these allegorical transformations and expresses the emotional states of the characters is admirably suited to opera; it is also close to Auden's transparent light verse. The ballads of the whores and roaring boys (36-41, 48-49, 55-58), for instance, follow directly in the folk-song tradition of "As I walked out one evening" (see above, p. 130ff.). The imagery is necessarily uncomplicated for the sake of an audience who will probably hear the words only once. Short lines and pointed riming similarly assist the audience's comprehension and emphasize the didactic point. For example, Nick Shadow, the devil, sings in his epilogue: "Many insist I do not exist./ At times I wish I didn't."[31] The riddling common in Auden's mature poetry would be out of place in an aria so the librettists have limited such devices as *double-entendre* to the prose *recitativo secco*. When Nick Shadow appears to announce Tom's inheritance from an unremembered "uncle," for instance, his description of the uncle depicts the devil as well as a believably human person. He is "one long parted from his native land" (18), whom Nick has served for many years. He had served in many trades, "all to his profit." "Sick for his home, sick for a memory of pleasure or of love," he has thought

[31] *The Rake's Progress*, 236. Naturally, the effectiveness in performance of such pointed riming depends greatly on the articulation of the singers.

that he would offer pleasure to an eager youth. If the
audience does not catch the covert references to the devil
in this recitative, Nick soon makes his identity plain when
he announces that the progress of a rake is beginning.

While the poetry is appropriate to the circumstances of
opera and effective in articulating the didactic theme, it
is also consonant with the eighteenth-century setting. Not
only are most arias rimed in couplets, but the imagery in
which the characters express their thoughts is characteristically neo-Classical. When Tom envisions a heaven
on earth, he does not speak in Marxist utopian terms, but
refers to man's rising through the Chain of Being to the
top. When the librettists want to present Anne as an
angel, they rely on the precedent of neo-Classical usage in
calling her a Venus. In fact, the entire theme of the opera
is implicit in its development of three different conceptions of Venus, all of them appropriate to the eighteenth-
century cultural setting. The first is the pastoral Venus to
whom Tom and Anne dedicate themselves while they are
still in the garden; the second, the bawdy Venus endorsed
by the whores; and the third, the Heavenly Venus whom
Anne portrays in Bedlam.[32] Part of the usefulness of the
neo-Classical imagery, which might seem simply outworn
in a non-operatic modern poem, is that a representative
of Heaven can be introduced indirectly and dramatically.
More important, the use of eighteenth-century imagery
allows a poetry which, besides its obvious universal im-

---

[32] These three versions of love correspond to Kierkegaard's three
categories: the aesthetic, the ethical, and the religious. Monroe
Spears rightly points out two versions of the Absurd in Tom's
progress. First is the worldly and false Absurd implicit in his marriage to Baba; second is the true Absurd embodied in his leap
of faith in the redeeming power of Love when he renames the
Queen of Hearts as the third card.

plications, has the same historical roots as both the setting and Stravinsky's modern neo-Classical music.

In many ways *The Rake's Progress* is a showcase of Auden's poetic mode. He has produced many other works of comparable value within their genres, but in the opera he seems to have found a set of conventions that is most congenial to his poetic and dramatic talents. He has been able to develop an allegorized moral fable that is dramatically effective while utilizing his skill with the sung ballad and lyric. Opera also provides a form in which over-life-sized characters and unrealistic tableau plots are entirely appropriate, and in which states of mind endowed with emotional immediacy through song are more relevant than strongly individualized characters. In addition, the highly artificial nature of operatic conventions can emphasize the distinction between art and life. At the same time, his mature view of man as willful actor can be forcefully demonstrated through the medium of music and words. In short, important characteristics of Auden's poetry which are sometimes limitations are, in this medium, assets. Not only is *The Rake's Progress* a fine operatic poem; it can also be seen as an epitome of Auden's mature poetic mode.

CHAPTER VII

CRITICAL CONCLUSIONS

WITH the scope of Auden's poetry brought into focus, we are equipped to attempt a tentative assessment of his work as a whole—to estimate the shape of his talent, its particular virtues and limitations. At the outset, however, we must be willing to accept Auden's characteristic mode as legitimate for a poetry. If we are less than wholeheartedly receptive to Auden's kind of poetry, we run the risk of prejudging his work by our own expectations of what it ought to be. The neo-Romantic reading of Auden, exemplified at its best by John Bayley and at its weakest by Joseph Warren Beach, provides a case in point. In the negative sense that he early began reacting against Romantic aesthetic principles (and analogous impulses in himself), Auden has written under their influence. But the neo-Romantic approach can engage Auden's poetry only through what he has attempted to avoid. Similarly, any critical approach which devalues allegory as a form of poetic expression must slight the distinctive qualities of some of Auden's best work. At least at this point in his career, only his own intentions offer sure entry into his poetry.

To categorize Auden's own aims, even "anti-Romantic" seems at the last too restrictive a term. While this study has shown how many of his poetic practices are most easily conceived as reactions against Romanticism, Auden has accomplished more than simply negating the Romantic celebration of the poet's unique personality. In the perspective of a highly productive thirty-five years, Auden emerges as a traditional poet in the most profound sense.

He again and again demonstrates the relevance to the modern world of the artistic and moral wisdom of the past. Like Stravinsky in music, he has revivified in modern context and idiom nearly all the traditional forms and genres of his art, many of them previously in disuse if not disfavor. Auden reaches back through all of English poetry, even to its roots in Anglo-Saxon and Icelandic. If T. S. Eliot, largely through the use of quotation and explicit allusion, has made the modern poet and reader conscious of standing at the head of a tradition, Auden, the second-generation modern, has accomplished a similar end through poetic forms and implicit allusion. Though Auden's career may have begun in relatively simple anti-Romanticism, it has grown into an affirmation of the larger artistic and moral tradition of the western world.

If for the moment we arbitrarily separate Auden's poems from their living context and look at them as self-contained structures of sound and meaning, we can see how his astounding versatility serves the purposes of a traditional poetry. Every poetic resource, be it a verse form, a set style, a rhetorical device, or a specialized idiom, has the potential power to call forth a new insight into the life of the present. A poet may choose to confine himself to a relatively narrow range of poetic resources in order to discover what they can show him in the successive experiences he encounters. Clearly Auden has made a different choice. He wants to try out what every poetic resource and every possible combination of poetic resources can mold out of the life of the present. As a deeply traditional poet, he can never be satisfied with a single style or a single kind of poem. Auden wants to compose every kind of poem, and he very nearly has. Even among the relatively few works this study has singled out for special consideration, his range of poetic strategy is imposing. A truer sense of his scope can be gained by reading seriatim through *The Collected Poetry*, limited though it is to works written by 1945. Auden's has been a sustained examination of our world through a complex series of prisms drawn from past poetries. As a result, not only can we now appreciate unsuspected beauties that he has drawn from familiar poetic elements, but we can measure our surroundings against a broader perspective that is as directly artistic as it is philosophic or religious. Auden has been the more effective for having long ago ceased to worry about stating profound or final truths in poetry. Instead he has concentrated on the ultimately more fruitful goal of perfecting each new amalgamation of poetic resources with human experience.

Naturally Auden is not always at his best and if his shorter poems tend towards any particular fault, a number, like "Metalogue to the Magic Flute" (1960), lack economy. The easily expandable structure we have noted in "As I walked out one evening" can lure the poet into including unnecessarily reiterative images and stanzas. In general, Auden seems at his best when the demands on his imagination are most stringent. The more exacting the requirements on his imagination, the more likely he is to produce a truly memorable poem, in which sound and meaning serve each other so intimately that no waste motion is possible.

Auden's longer poems raise a different sort of problem. Perhaps because they are constructed out of shorter set pieces that could stand alone, they often fail to form a proportioned whole. Even his plays are not dramatically exciting. Like many of his longer works, they are structural equivalents of Goethe's *Faust*, which, in turn, is much like opera. And as in *Faust*, as Auden himself describes it, scenes could be added or removed without producing a radical change.[1] The kind of unity Auden achieves in his best long poems can best be illustrated by "The Sea and the Mirror," which maintains a strict formal relatedness between tableaux-poems.[2] In the end I think we must agree with F. W. Dupee and John Bradbury in describing Auden's as essentially a lyric talent which is at its best in sustaining poetic effects within a relatively short space.[3]

Auden's technical mastery over language and his knowledge of and debt to the poetic tradition have already been widely acknowledged. We must go beyond viewing poems in isolation to examine the relation of his work to the larger human world outside it, to assess what we may call his "vision." One of Auden's recent descriptions of "authentic" poetry may be helpful: "To be authentic, a work of art must exhibit two contradictory qualities, the quality of always-ness and quality of now-ness. It must remain of permanent significance to later generations, whatever historical changes may occur, and it must have the uniqueness which comes from being made by a unique human being at a unique point in time. If it lacks always-ness it is merely a fashionable entertainment. . . ; if it lacks now-ness it lacks life."[4]

Obviously, we in the present cannot predict with any

[1] See *DH*, 115.

[2] This judgment is by now almost a critical commonplace. A recent concurrence and list of earlier proponents of the same view appears in Frederick P. W. MacDowell's " 'The Situation of Our Time': Auden in His American Phase," in *Aspects of American Poetry*, ed. Richard M. Ludwig (Columbus, Ohio, 1962), 243.

[3] See, respectively, "Auden and Others," *Nation*, CLX (May 26, 1945), 605, and "Auden and the Tradition," *Western Review*, XII (Summer 1948), 229. Another important exception to this generalization is, as I have indicated earlier, *The Rake's Progress*.

[4] "The Problem of Nowness," *The Mid-Century*, No. 19 (November 1960), 17.

certainty the reactions of future readers, but clearly Auden's vision does reach to the levels of timeless concern that have moved readers in the past. He is able to tap reservoirs of universal imagery in dreams, folktales, and mythology. He encompasses, either explicitly or by implication, the basic philosophic and religious insights of western culture. His ability to elucidate the broad implications of particular events or human types places him, at least potentially, in the great tradition of moral and philosophic poets whose vision probes the nature of human nature.

Many critics have pointed out Auden's thoughtful scrutiny and forceful analysis of the major ideologies of western civilization. Some have gone on, however, to find his poetry uncertain or indecisive in its final disposition. If Auden only had something to say, the line goes, he might be great instead of merely good. Auden's poetic impersonality probably encourages this response, as does his related tendency to articulate his vision by negations. He is an *anti*-Romantic. He perceives Divine Truth through "*negative* knowledge." The only ulterior purpose of poetry is "by telling the truth, to *dis*enchant and to *dis*intoxicate."[5] Auden's indirection, however, does not grow from uncertainty of commitment. Since his reconversion about 1940, Christianity has provided him with a conceptual and, perhaps to a lesser extent, an emotional framework that has guided his thought and his life. His indirection reflects a profound moralist's distrust of moral codes. He is acutely conscious of the ease with which human beings can convert any specific moral platform into fascism or Holy War. To avoid such corruptions, Auden, like the greatest Christian moralists before him, requires each man to accept personal responsibility for his

[5] *DH*, 27; my italics.

own living enactment of Love. Love as a moral principle differs markedly in kind from a moral code, because no one can predetermine what will be a Loving action in a given situation. Each individual must determine his own course of action. Hence Auden insists again and again on the importance of self-critical examination of one's motives and desires. Auden's commitment to the moral principle of Love lies at the root of his didactic strategies in poetry and undergirds his mature view of the world. His vision seems to lack a positive program at times primarily because it requires so much thoughtful and independent moral reflection from every individual who would take his poetry seriously. All his readers, just because they are human, will share one characteristic: all will want to avoid naked self-encounter.

Auden's "now-ness" we are in a better position to estimate. The danger of universally applicable insights is that they may seem unrelated to any particular time or place and hence fail to make contact with the reader. Indeed, most of Auden's mature poetry has inclined toward allegory, which is particularly liable to this fault. His characters appear not as recognizably complex human beings, but as personified human types or philosophical attitudes. His landscapes are ordered not by Nature, but by an Intelligence that finds its abstract concepts made palpable in mountains, lakes, or streams. Auden's poems sparkle with striking particulars, but his images derive their aptness from the precision and, frequently, the unexpectedness with which they embody an idea. The "now-ness" that Auden achieves, then, is not based on a new insight into what the world around him can mean, but on a new perception of the immediacy and relevance of a generalized human attitude or concept. This allegorical habit of mind has cut Auden off from the kind of poetic particularity that has been most often admired in this century. Allegory, however, has received less respect than it deserves, as Auden's character types, at their best, can demonstrate. For example, the power of his insight and his control over rhetoric have enabled him to particularize for all time, as it were, two antipodal aberrations of mind which every human being must fear in others and in himself. One is embodied in the self-appointed divine scourge of the world (most notably the Vicar in *The Dog Beneath the Skin*) and the other, in the self-defeated disciple of progress who, out of his lack of spiritual commitment, cannot perform any significant action (Herod in *For the Time Being*).

"Now-ness," as Auden describes it, is a quality a poem derives from being the product of a unique person at a unique moment in time, but his own poems, as we have seen, refuse to assert his personal uniqueness. By avoiding a recognizably individual style and by presenting his poems impersonally, Auden has separated his work from the usual ways of identifying a unique vision. His poems as much as those of any other poet are the products of a particular individual, but he does not ask acceptance of his vision because it is unique or because it is his. The vision of humanity articulated in his poems, he seems to imply, would be available to any perceptive and rigorously honest pair of eyes. To put it another way, Auden's reader is rarely allowed the comfortable feeling that the poem puts him in contact with a fellow human being who is revealing his innermost feelings. Instead, the reader is confronted with a verbal mirror which lays bare some aspect of his human nature. Usually the sight is anything but comforting. Auden has found poetry a discipline which measures and controls his impulses; he asks the reader as well to ponder self-critically what "the luck of verbal playing" reveals of his hidden nature.

The combination of Auden's impersonal presentation of poetry and his serious moral and didactic purpose in writing it places him in a paradoxical situation. He very rightly rejects the self-assertion implicit in preaching at the reader. Yet Auden wants to lead his reader to measure himself against the mirror of the poem, not to treat it simply as an aesthetic performance. The resources available to the poet to trap the reader, such as satire, the rhetorical pyrotechnics of riddling, or the upsetting of a reader's nostalgia, all have one great disadvantage. While they may direct the reader toward the unflattering reflection of himself, every additional complexity in the poetic performance makes it easier for him to feel satisfied with himself for perceiving that brilliance of technique. The artifice of Auden's poetry reflects his consciousness of himself as an actor and his desire to lead the reader to similar self-awareness. The same artifice, unfortunately, offers the reader a way to escape real self-examination, not merely by understanding the ingenious mechanics of the trap, but by entertaining satisfaction at his power to do so. In fact, an awareness of such a paradox may have supported Auden's recent views on the impossibility of being serious in poetry.

Auden's versatile inventiveness in poetic artifice has filled the stage in this study, perhaps to a fault. Auden himself reminds us that "since the creation of a work of art is, in the artist's experience, a conscious act, . . . the artist is inclined to overstress the conscious elements in his work, while the uncreative reader overstresses the unconscious element. The romantic aesthetic is a reader's

[192]

aesthetic."[6] Perhaps through adopting, wherever possible, Auden's own perspective, this study has erred on the side of describing his poems as if they were entirely the result of conscious strategies. Clearly Auden is more than simply a deft logician in verse, as the memorability and human relevance of his lines attest. Lines and whole passages stick in the back of the mind till a human situation recalls them to consciousness—to the mutual enrichment of the poetry and the experience. The arresting aphoristic quality of many lines results from the polished craftsmanship of an accomplished poet, but also his search for self-critical insights has yielded fruitful ambiguities and paradoxes which can open up direct inroads to a reader's deepest self. Auden's continual quest to transcend the present limits of conscious awareness is implicit not only in his themes but in his methods of composition. In effect, Auden seems to compose in two stages. First is poetic playing with language which aims at uncovering new human insights. In this stage, the demands of verse form and unserious technique seem notable aids to help Auden gain imaginative freedom from his conscious thoughts. In the second stage, after the intuitive search has yielded new insights, Auden's conscious critical faculties must approve and perhaps readjust the protopoem.

Auden has been particularly acute in anticipating his reader's response and then gauging the most effective final disposition of poetic raw material. His alertness to his audience is manifested in his periodic revisions of poems and titles and his use of editorial devices to modify the context in which a poem is presented to the reader. He is remarkable among poets in the extent to which

[6] "Mimesis and Allegory," *English Institute Annual*, 1940, ed. Rudolf Kirk (New York, 1941), 4-5.

he is actively concerned with the reader's perspective on what he writes. Outside his own poems, his catholic taste and acuity of insight as a reader assure him a high place in the long line of distinguished poet-critics in English.

Whatever the final impact of Auden's poetry, he has established an admirable model for literature in at least one respect. Despite the difficulties inherent in our amorphous culture, he has insisted on the necessity of re-establishing contact with the world outside one's own subjectivity. His success in bringing his private vision into contact with the public world has demonstrated that poetry need not abandon even such a world as we live in.

In his poem on Yeats, Auden speaks of the relation between the poet and his language in a most significant manner. He describes the poet not as one who lives by language, but as one by whom languages lives. Just so, it is Auden's ability to give life to language that will assure his being read. If, years hence, the vision expressed in Auden's poetry fails to move the readers of the future, the virtuosity and versatility of his power with language may lead him to be treated as a poet's poet, as Spenser frequently has been. For the present his vision at its best achieves the rare virtue of illuminating profoundly our condition as individual human beings and as a civilization.

BIBLIOGRAPHICAL NOTE

STUDENTS of Auden are blessed with excellent bibliographical resources. An invaluable aid to research is Edward Callan's *Annotated Check List of the Works of W. H. Auden*, originally published in *Twentieth Century Literature*, IV (April-July, 1958), 30-50. Monroe K. Spears, in his *Poetry of Auden*, supplements the list and carries it forward through 1962. Spears also compiles a useful index of Auden's published poems by title and by first line; the latter listing summarizes the printing history of each poem. The British scholar, B. C. Bloomfield, has recently published the definitive *W. H. Auden, A Bibliography, The Early Years Through 1955* (University of Virginia Press, 1964). This full-scale bibliography includes much useful information, including lists of selected reviews of Auden's volumes and a list of criticism up to and somewhat beyond 1955. Most of the essays in this list, as Bloomfield points out, fail to be memorable. The anthology of critical articles edited by Monroe K. Spears (*Auden*, Prentice-Hall: Twentieth Century Views Series, 1964) brings together much of the good criticism on Auden and also includes a short bibliography of additional commentaries.

APPENDIX: AUDEN WORKS CITED

I. *Poems and Prose Poems*

[197]

II. *Plays and Libretti*

III. *Essays and Criticism*

APPENDIX

[201]

INDEX

Absurd, the, 51; in *The Rake's Progress*, 183n
acte gratuit, 170
aestheticism, 11-12, 52
allegory, in Auden, 7, 16, 74-78, 185; purpose, 8, 90; as control on emotions, 30, 69-70; as habit of mind, 32, 74, 190-91; types of, 74-78; defined, 75, 75n, 77; imagery in, 76-78, 87; theme in, 77; devices, 86, 86n, 90; and occasional poetry, 94; and semidrama, 118-19; and opera, 184
Anglo-Saxon poetry, 15, 17; and Auden, 186
Ansen, Alan, 155n
anti-Romanticism. *See* Auden, W. H.
anxiety, 50
art and the artist, function of art, 27, 39; art as artifice, 12, 144-46, 162; nature of the artist, 30, 37, 107, 108; art as a guide to life, 39-40, 118; frivolity of art, 41-42; nature of, 51, 81, 108, 188; the work of art, 107; as contraption, 115; now-ness in, 190-92
art and life, 108, 115-17; personal feelings in, 20; separation of, 40, 114; art as magic, 51, 108-09, 114, 117; as mirror, 60-61, 108, 191-92; as play, 140; highbrow and lowbrow, 129-30, 141n
AUDEN, W. H.
   biography: English period, 3; American period, 3, 15n; Oxford, 13, 16, 19, 27-28, 38, 69; Icelandic background, 17; early writings, 17; collaboration with Isherwood, 18; early career, 21-23, 27; early

romanticism, 21, 26, 41, 66-69; maturity, 26, 49, 52-54, 55, 144, 187, 188-92; childhood and youth, 26, 65, 68; collaboration with Kallman, 155n; with Stravinsky, 157
   intellectual development: religious profession, 3-4, 118n, 138; reconversion to Christianity, 3-4, 49-51, 103, 189; social attitudes, 3, 22, 23n, 67, 72; Christianity, 3, 50, 53, 55, 70, 71; philosophical position, 4, 12; political position, 4, 22, 69; development of characteristic mode, 12, 21, 25-27, 47, 54; of anti-Romanticism, 20-21, 26-27, 30, 35, 93, 113; politics and the poet, 22, 31, 38, 42; Marxism, 22-23; Freudian psychology, 69; orthodoxy, 69; interest in opera, 155
   the Auden manner: variety and virtuosity, 4, 5-6, 12, 17, 26, 124-25; literary strategies, 6, 7, 12, 14, 185; modern tone, 11-13; audience, 21; development, 21, 25-26; obscurity, 25-26, 28-29; diction, 126-27; unseriousness, 138, 141, 157
   the Auden mode: 6, 8, 11, 13, 21, 34, 64; indirection, 5, 12, 13, 25, 76-77; integrality, 6, 12, 20, 72, 103-05; impersonality, 7, 19-20, 123; paradox of, 13, 144, 192; detachment, 19, 68; self-awareness, 20, 21, 41, 69, 76, 152; and modern critics, 30, 32; ambiguity in, 31, 75, 138, 193
   special concepts and bi-